KLARA KHARKOV LIFE

Michael Blekhman and Olga Bezhanova

Copyright © 2022 by Michael Blekhman and Olga Bezhanova.

ISBN- 978-1-68506-018-3 (sc)
ISBN- 978-1-68506-041-1 (hc)

All rights reserved. No part of this book may be reproduced or transmitted in any form or by any means, electronic or mechanical, including photocopying, recording, or by any information storage and retrieval system, without permission in writing from the copyright owners.

The views expressed in this work are solely those of the authors and do not necessarily reflect the views of the publisher, and the publisher hereby disclaims any responsibility for them.

InfusedMedia Co. LLC
www.infusedmedia.co
1-888-251-6088

To those people whom, God willing, I will once live up to.

I

There were so many shooting stars in the sky that I ran out of things to wish on them. Someone shook them off his big, cold hand and they started descending quietly, creating sleepy, sugary snow mounds or writing on my window-pane funny and complex symbols of an unknown alphabet. It was as if that same someone used them to wish merry Christmas to our city and after that decided to find his reflection in my window, look into my notebook, and read the last lines of my recently finished novel.

"Who first called it a snowfall?" I reflected, striving to decipher the main idea behind these symbols. What was the connection between them and my novel? Were they each other's reflection or did they represent two different alphabets of the same language?

"A snowfall?" I asked myself, crestfallen. "Is that how snow falls? Or is it, rather, what it feels like when things befall you? Or when you fall for a cold-hearted woman? Or when a friend's coldness causes your downfall? Or when a critic lets the gavel fall – more on his work than on mine? But actual snow doesn't fall like this at all."

"But if it weren't for my notebook, would you make any sense at all?"

"Anyways, why am I talking to you about sense? In the place you descended from this is hopefully a lot better understood, even though – and this is what I fear - in a completely different way."

"Then who needs this alphabet of mine if you have one of your own? And you will always descend, regardless of my wishes."

". . . And you will keep descending onto the city that just celebrated Christmas and is preparing for New Year's – an entirely new year. . ."

". . . Not even noticing that in the new year there will be someone completely different on this side of the window from the person who was here before. And you will not even inquire where the one who was here before went."

Is there anything else I can say in my notebook that you haven't heard before? Anything you haven't seen and haven't touched yet?

I sighed, rapped my fingers on the notebook's cover which still didn't bear the name of my novel, opened the notebook on a random page, on a Roman numeral, and looked out of the window once again.

"In any case, you are here, even though you are on the other side of the window, since a window doesn't exist for you. Let it be non-existent for me as well, then you will be able to translate the contents of my notebook into your other-worldly – or not? – language."

". . . And we will find a name for my novel together."

If you came here to see me, it means my downfall can be postponed. In case, of course, the window doesn't suggest a different kind of fall. . ."

"You see, and I almost lost all hope."

Books were staring at me out of bookcases, trying to catch a glimpse of what my still nameless notebook contained. The notebook was filled with words that were hardly capable of saying anything and with the almost meaningless Roman numerals.

Books were staring out of bookcases: the old volume in a mother-of-pearl cover that was deciphered for me but not by me, as well as these, my favorite ones, which don't help me but at least – and most importantly – they don't get in the way. And this one. . . I still don't understand its role completely but by the time my notebook is finished I hope I will. . . Otherwise, writing in my notebook would have been a risky business and who even knows if it would have been justified? . .

Still, was I the one who wrote it? I was looking past my notebook and thinking that, of course, it had already existed and all I had to do was find it. So I set out in search of it – like the medieval Admiral who set out in the search of an old world that turned out to be a completely new one.

"I must be more fortunate than many of my fellow-explorers because I did find it and now the only thing my notebook lacks in order to become a book is a title," I thought contentedly. Of course, I could leave it as is. If one can write a poem without a protagonist, why can't one write a novel without a title?

No, I should still give a name to my novel. I will definitely give it a name and they will help me since I have removed this window that has been separating us.

Otherwise, how will a cold-hearted woman, a cold-blooded enemy and a cool-headed critic manage to decide for themselves and inform the world that my notebook doesn't deserve to be read? If the author has a name and his work has a specific title, it is easy to say that nothing else needs to be known. In the absence of a name and a title, though, one will have to read the book in order to be able to proclaim that it is not worth reading.

It's true that often a novel's beginning is so similar to a title as to replace it. . . My novel, however, needs a title because its opening lines don't substitute or predict it. They actually do the exact opposite.

At first, the city prepares for New Year's and only after ringing it in it will start getting ready for Christmas. Instead of making wishes at a speed matching that of the shooting stars falling on her city, she kept thinking that, in all truth, she had no more wishes left to make. And if old-fashioned snow stars descended onto the city instead of the usual gloomy haze, there would be nothing for her to wish on them.

"It's funny," she thought while she was getting into a trolley and checking perfunctorily on her handbag. "It's funny how nature helps those who have nothing else to wish for. If I had any more wishes, shooting stars would have come at once."

She was lucky in that the trolley was almost empty and her usual seat was free.

"Turns out I did have a wish," she smiled and pressed herself against the window that protected her from the street. Now, she could look more calmly at the hospital and its fence which remained behind the closing doors and the locked windows of the trolley.

"I remember the wish I wanted to make."

She opened a book that looked exactly like my notebook although it seemed to have a title already. She took it everywhere she went. Every now and then, she looked out of the window without really interrupting her reading. She liked seeing snow mounds that looked incredibly similar to cotton wool and that could have fallen off from a huge Christmas tree right before that. The frozen, eggnog-colored lamplights looked drab against this background.

"Or is that eggnog?" she asked herself sternly but had no time to think of an answer since she noticed a couple walking towards the hospital at an uneven pace. Samuil's face was the same color as these unnatural snow mounds. Klara was moaning and trying to bend to the ground. Her full-term pregnancy was getting in the way, even as it was the only thing that kept her grounded.

"I need to rest!" she moaned, sitting down in a heap of snow.

"Klara, my love," said Samuil while trying to raise her. "You'll catch a cold, let's go, we are so close already."

They would get up and walk several more steps before she subsided into the snow again in order to catch her breath even though the breath refused to be caught. As bad luck might have it, Klara had gone into labor in the small hours when not only a cab was impossible to find but even hitching a ride on a road that was incredibly white for such a dark time of the night was out of the question. So they set off on foot towards the maternity ward.

They had been walking for over an hour, stopping, sitting down, and getting up again. The snow was blinding them, but Klara's vision had clouded over back home when she tried to get dressed and her back felt like it was crumbling into pieces in the manner of a stale bagel. The pain made both walking and sitting equally impossible. Klara's fur-coat kept her warm but its weight kept dragging her down into the snow mound and the only thing she wanted was to give birth already and finally go to sleep, not having to think about giving birth any more. Inside her furry mittens, her fingers were sweaty and so swollen that she couldn't clench her fist any more. Her kerchief slid away and for the first time in her life she felt wrinkles gathering on her forehead. If she could see herself in the mirror, she would be terrified of this change in her appearance. Now, however, she had no energy left to feel fear just like that time when she was drowning in the Dnieper all those years ago.

"God, when will the baby finally come?!" I moaned while clutching Senya's hand and subsiding into a temptingly warm snow mound. "Poor women, why do they suffer so?! . . Jesus, why do I say 'they' if I'm one of them?"

He was on the verge of tears and as he was kissing my mittened hands, he tried raising me out of the snow mound.

"Klarochka," he was saying, "let's go, we are really close. When we get there they will help you undress, get this stupid fur-coat off you. . ."

"And everything else, too!" I gasped, not even trying to get up because the pain was more than I could bear and I had no more energy to keep bearing it.

"Of course, they will take everything off, just like they should, and you'll forget ever dragging all this heavy stuff around. They'll give you some medication, put you on a comfortable table, you'll make one last effort, and give us a son or a daughter."

"A son!" I barked confidently, getting up almost in spite of myself.

"A son!" she told me in a whisper but firmly.

"A son!" rang out in the trolley through the closed window.

And Klara strode to give birth to a son, strode instead of trudging.

Or rather, they strode together, as usual.

II

Now Klara temporarily forgot - how could any one remember anything any more? - that she strove, or rather dreamt, of getting past New Year's. There were many reasons for that but the main was to delay her son's enlistment for a year. In any case, one was always better off being considered born a year later, of course, just considered.

"And what if it's a girl?" asked or maybe just said Maria Isaakovna, with a barely perceptible hint of sarcasm.

"Mama, such things don't just happen," Klara answered reassuringly and went back to her Roman Law textbook. Professor Fuks delivered his lectures as well as any famous actor would, let alone any Roman tribune. So many students gathered to hear his lectures that not only was there no room to swing a cat but even the tiniest kitten could hardly be swung in the lecture-hall. Passing Fuks's final exam, especially while being pregnant, was harder than conquering the Roman Empire. Klara, however, never doubted herself and neither did Samuil. Vladimir Fedorovich didn't doubt her either, although when Maria Isaakovna spoke, he remained mostly silent and sometimes smiled, albeit not sarcastically but in agreement.

"Volodia, why do you keep smiling?" Maria Isaakovna asked in a voice of a temporarily dethroned empress. "No, this man will drive me crazy one day! A serious issue is being discussed, and he's sitting here like nothing's happening and keeps smiling. Volodia, stop smiling right now! I'm talking to you!"

"What do you think I should do, cry?" Vladimir Fedorovich smiled broadly and shrugged his shoulders.

How can one be expected not to smile if the war has been over for six and a half years, and even though they share their apartment with neighbors, it's still better than some shack in the evacuation to the Ural Mountains, everybody is healthy and sound, and the ration cards are no longer in use, Samuil is about to graduate from medical school and Klara from law school? And I will soon have a grandson, or maybe a granddaughter, which is just as well, even though Klara is certain she will have a boy. Should this make one cry, or what?

"This issue isn't being discussed, Mama," Klara observed without raising her eyes from her notes, written in a soft, leftward-sloping handwriting. "This issue was resolved a long time ago. I can remember the approximate date this issue was resolved and even the time of day or, rather, night. Of course, I can't be completely sure about that since the occasion was both solemn and significant."

Even though she stopped short of clarifying what the occasion in question was, her statement made an impression. Samuil was the only one who was one hundred per cent content with it, given that he was in possession of all the facts, which allowed him to admire the precision of his wife's description. Vladimir Fedorovich smiled again, while Maria Isaakovna flashed like a lightning in response to Klara's comment, Vladimir Fedorovich's smile, and Samuil's contented thoughtfulness.

III

Before the war, Klara, Maria Isaakovna and Vladimir Fedorovich lived in a privileged two-bedroom apartment that, of course, they didn't have to share with any neighbors. It was located in what was maybe the coziest neighborhood of Kharkov, called Nagorny neighborhood. Maria Isaakovna worked as a construction engineer. She supervised extremely important construction projects and designed huge power plants at Lakes Sevan and Balkhash, and in many other parts of the Soviet Union.

Maria had been born in Byelorussia in a Dnieper shtetl called Rechitsa.

Her real name was Mary and not Maria, but Mary sounded too British, which made little sense when one was from Rechitsa. Isaak, her father, was the best cabinet-maker in the entire province, while her mother, Klara, was considered illiterate and had given birth to eight children. It was true that she didn't know her letters but that hardly made her illiterate. It was just that she had no time to learn, what with eight children and a husband permanently stuck in his cabinet-making workshop.

Still, she was smarter than many of those who knew how to read and write. People from all over the shtetl came to her for advice, just like they did to Sancho Panza on his island. The advice she dispensed was very good. Not once in her life was she known to offer a bad piece of advice.

Among her eight children, there were two girls - Mary and Haya, the rest were boys who - once they grew up - became socialists and died. That is, some of them died because they were socialists, while the others died in the war, which had nothing to do with them being socialists.

One of Mary's brothers turned out to be a mathematician. He proved a theorem that couldn't be proven. Or, rather, aided by his very Jewish spirit of contradiction so disliked by many, he disproved an axiom. Of course, it wasn't really an axiom since if it were one nobody could have disproven it. Aaron disagreed it was an axiom and this allowed him to prove it wrong. The Imperial Academy of Sciences in St. Petersburg appreciated his outstanding capabilities and awarded him a silver medal on the condition that he would change his unscientific Jewish name of Aaron into a more Russian-sounding Arkadi. His last name, Krupetsky, sounded almost like the aristocratic Russian family names of Obolensky or even Golitsynsky. If only, of course, one could forget about needless particularities.

Her older siblings were always busy, so Mary learned to entertain herself. When she was little, she went to the Dnieper which was so wide it touched the horizon. Only an inexperienced and excessively romantic observer could perceive this river as tranquil in a calm weather (to use Gogol's famed line). In reality, even next to the river-banks there were scores of pits and breakers. One can only imagine how many there were in the middle of the river, which Mary's four-year-old height barely permitted her to see.

Nobody had taught Mary to fear the river. Nobody had taught her anything except reading and writing but these skills turned out to be useless in dealing with the river. So she entered the water just like she entered her father's workshop to stare at a new cabinet and holiday chairs or her mother's kitchen to try knodel, latkes, or gefilte fish. She had no idea she could drown because she didn't know what drowning was. This is why Mary just started swimming and discovered she liked it. Eventually, she learned to cross the Dnieper and walk on the opposite bank which turned out to be just as ordinary, that is, just as amazing, as her bank where she was born. Then, she would come home by dinner-time.

Klara, as they would later discover, followed in her mother's footsteps. Once, when they were visiting Rechitsa, she also decided to visit the Dnieper, see what it was like, and take a swim. She was six years old but she still had no idea that in order to swim one had to know how to do it. So she simply ran away and went to the Dnieper, especially since it was so close to her grandparents' house. Nobody noticed her leaving. A child wandering off on her own was no big deal in Rechitsa. Pogroms had been long gone, the war long over, and there wasn't as much as a cloud in sight. Klara ran to the river, enjoying life and singing "Stand up, damned of the Earth", and threw herself into that water that seemed as harmless as fresh soup in her Nana's old bowl. The river was lots of fun until suddenly its bottom fell through and Klara went under.

She managed to come up for air a couple of times but every gasp of air required more effort than the one before. In the end, she had no more energy to come up and decided to stop trying since it was useless anyways. And then I realized how upset Mom would be when she finds out I drowned, so I decided to emerge from the water one more time, just for her sake.

This was when she was noticed by a young sailor who lived nearby and had just come to the river-bank to take a swim. Without even taking his clothes off, he jumped in the river, dragged the brave girl out, and took her to Maria. Mom still got upset but I can only imagine how heart-broken she would have been, had I actually drowned. This just goes to show that one should always try to come up for air one last time. Who knows, maybe help is on the way at that very moment.

IV

Mary was beautiful, with thick dark hair, huge, slightly protruding eyes, and a touch of condescension in her smile.

At the age of sixteen, she married Zinovi Stolberg, an energetic, intelligent and enterprising young man. Three years later, in 1929, she gave birth to Klara and left her husband because he annoyed her with his opinions. Not his opinions as such since she never listened to what he said anyways but, rather, with his having the gall to express opinions.

Of course, Zinovi was Zinovi just as much as Aaron was Arkadi. His real name was Zalman, so Klara was in reality Klara Zalmanovna instead of Clarissa Zinovievna, as she started introducing herself later in life. Zinovi had planned to call her Elena, but having opinions turned out to be a bad idea for him. Maria ended up following her own rule that a son should be given his grandfather's name, while a daughter should be named after her grandmother.

After the divorce and before the war began, Zinovi sometimes saw Klara but it happened so rarely that she felt she almost never met him at all.

In Kharkov, which was the first Ukrainian capital city after the revolution, Maria entered an engineering program and became its best student. That was no surprise because a person who can come out a winner from a struggle with the Dnieper will not be defeated by anything that can happen on even the most challenging stretch of land.

Arguing with her was impossible or, rather, it was completely useless. Her logic and her way of constructing an argument were more than ironclad, they were made of some yet-to-be-discovered refractory substance. Maria's classmates, who were mostly Civil War veterans, used to say she had a male brain. Still, she was a woman. With a braid encircling her head, huge eyes, and the capacity to cross any river, no matter how challenging the task might be to any self-proclaimed hero.

Every morning, Maria would walk from her apartment in Pushkin Entry to Sumskaya Street, smiling at the soaring golden Engineering House, and the bright grey Gosprom skyscraper, and the rising building of the Ukrainian Government in the endless – as endless as her entire life – Dzerzhinsky Square. Her life was only about to begin, and the world's best monument to the poet Taras Shevchenko wasn't there yet, just like the Glass Fountain wasn't there, and she had no way of knowing that it was going to resemble her chiffon scarf.

Her heels clicked against the obedient paving stone and the timid asphalt, in her brief-case she had her homework, which was the best in her cohort, and in her blueprint tube she carried the best drawings of anybody in her program. The Sumskaya Street, endless in its regal flow, moved past her towards the tsarist buildings, the Salamander House, the imposing bank building, the Pushkin Square, and the festive Ukrainian theater. Then, it joined the Nikolaevskaya Square, where buildings designed before the war by the famous Professor Beketov winked at Maria with their crystal-clear windows. Lower down, she could see a tranquil grey no-frills building constructed as recently as 1925.

On weekends, Maria would leave Nikolaevskaya Square and walk down the prideful Pushkin Street, which at that time one couldn't even imagine crossed by trams or railways. She would pass by the churches that made the street look the wife of a merchant guild's honorary member. Then on to the buildings designed by the famous architect Beketov, which reminded her of a string of Christmas lights or October fireworks and which made the street look as aristocratic as it so richly deserved. She would return to her own Pushkin Entry to prepare for class, read, draw, and wield her slide rule.

And, of course, to come out to the balcony with Klara to stare into the skies that had blessed them with the miracle of their endlessly happy lives.

V

Maria had scores of faithful admirers, which interested her little, since every would-be lover had the gall or the misfortune to have his own opinion about something. This must have been the admirers' way of asserting their male essence. Maria was more than happy with relying on her own essence, which was female. The only man she allowed to receive and adopt her opinions faithfully and without questioning was Vladimir Fedorovich, and this was what interested her about him. He was older, but she never felt the age difference. Anyways, six years were nothing to speak of.

Vladimir had been born in Warsaw when Poland was still part of the Russian Empire. He was a clerk. His job consisted of auditing the meat-packing and the produce-growing companies. For a while, he worked as an accountant for the Vtorchermet, then transferred to the Southern Railway Bureau, which was located in an imposing old building in the enormous Kharkov Railway Square. His supervisors admired how reliable and punctual he was.

He always knew how to locate the necessary paperwork simply because he never needed to search for any form or document. All paperwork that he wrote in a soft, straight handwriting without a single crossing out (when did Vladimir Petkevich ever make a cross out?) didn't need to be looked for since it was located in the right place at the right time - or, actually, any time one needed it.

When he was young, Vladimir was attracted to ballerinas, who were just as young. In his mature years, he fell in love with Mary, or, rather, he came to love her.

She allowed him to experience this feeling towards her only after making sure that he wasn't going to object to her about anything. He never even considered objecting because he loved Maria and Klara more than people normally know how to love others.

He also loved soccer. He didn't love playing it - that he didn't know how to do, - but he loved watching it. When Vladimir was twenty, Kharkov's team won the all-country championship, and he caught a glimpse of the famous players Privalov, Krotov, Norov, Kazakov, the Fomin brothers.

"In Odessa, in 1921," he would tell Klara, smiling, "Kazakov hit the crossbar, and it fell on the Odessa goalie's head. Can you imagine that?"

Maria didn't even shrug her shoulders because she was simply outraged about what he was teaching the child. Klara, however, wanted to see the crossbar fall, so she got interested in soccer. In the meanwhile, Vladimir Fedorovich got less and less passionate about soccer because after Privalov there was nobody who could play quite as well.

Vladimir couldn't swim, so when he was in the army he served as a coxswain of the launch. His slight frame didn't allow him to row but as a coxswain he was better than any one. He sat at the steer and kept count in a clear, loud voice, "One-two, one-two!"

I kept count to help the rowers set the speed. Once, near Phoros, which is close to Sevastopol, our launch got into the dead swells. Do you know what that means? On the surface, the water looks like glass, but underneath there are horrible swells, as if somebody were mixing the water in a shaker. Dead swells, may the devil take them, will not upset the launch, but it can cause one to fall asleep. One moment I was keeping count and then I was falling deep into sleep. If the rowers hadn't lost their rhythm and looked at me to see what was going on, I wouldn't be here right now. Of course, they lost the rhythm because I'd fallen asleep and stopped keeping count. They saved me from never waking up again.

Klara liked the story. It was even scarier than the one where the crossbar fell on the goalie's head.

After Maria graduated, she spent less time at home than on work-related trips, so Vladimir Fedorovich became Klara's primary caregiver. For him, this meant not intruding upon her growth and development and keeping watch over this process.

VI

In daycare, Klara was almost as much in charge as the adults. She didn't know why that happened and never thought about it. Everybody simply respected her opinion. Probably that happened because nobody but her actually had opinions, except, of course, the adults. She took the lead in all games (tag, hide-and-seek, anything), and she was never 'it', only when she really wanted to and not when it was her turn (when did Stolberg ever have a bad turn?)

At home she was happy, too, even more than simply happy. Klara would come home from daycare, and later from school, which turned out to be special, as special as their Pushkin Entry. She would rush into their amazing apartment that before Vladimir Fedorovich moved in was always empty. There were lots of delicious food, even caviar, but Mom was never there. She traveled for work: to Central Asia, the Caucasus, Siberia, Lake Baikal, the Crimea, Lake Balkhash, uranium mines. Maria Isaakovna would go from one place to another on a special small airplane. She was a high-class construction engineer who never had any conflicts with those who sent the airplane to fetch her: I never let myself overstep my bounds and never told anybody what I was doing, including about the uranium mines.

At home, Klara did endless homework, which she didn't dislike. She also had stamps, coins, and a white baby grand piano. There were hundreds or thousands of books that could be easier read than counted, as well. Klara learned to read the same way Maria learned to swim. Only, she was three, not four then. That's why she always had more fun at home than outside. Everywhere but at home she felt how much she missed her parents, which was something she hardly ever perceived when she was home because there she had the aura of the yearned-for eighteenth century, stamps with haughty Queen Victoria and King George who looked neither like Queen Victoria nor like each other, silver rubles of Peter the Great's and Tsar Nicholas's times.

Then Vladimir Fedorovich came into their lives, and things got better. He smiled, was always on her side, never got frazzled, let alone annoyed (when did Vladimir Fedorovich ever get annoyed?), and helped any way he could including coin and stamp collecting, the latter especially, even though I could never understand the fascination with all these useless kings and queens. Our stamps are a lot more interesting. Well, what can you expect from a child?

He took Klara to the Shevchenko Gardens, to the Pioneers' Palace to see the New Year's tree, and for all kinds of festive occasions. At the Pioneers' Palace she was once photographed with her gift, sitting in the lap of Postyshev, a high-ranking Soviet official, and Maria Isaakovna was very proud of this picture. Vladimir Fedorovich just smiled, and even though he said nothing, he kept thinking that it wasn't clear who should have been more proud.

He kept taking Klara around - to the beautiful Gorky Park and the endless Lesopark, down the Pushkinskaya Street that kept changing with every passing year, and the Basseinaya Street that was clanging with tram bells and thumping at the rail junctures, down the dreamy Chernyshevskaya Street.

VII

Rosa was from stetl close to Mariupol. Later on, Mariupol was named Zhdanov. Semen came from a city called Lipawa in Latvia, which was why Samuil knew a few words in Latvian. At the marketplace in Lipawa vendors always responded if one addressed them in Yiddish and especially if one talked Latvian. Still, Yiddish was very well-respected. If one spoke Russian, however, often nobody wanted to respond.

Semen's brothers left for Uruguay right after the revolution. There, they did well for themselves, started their own businesses. Moishe was the only one who came back to visit his mother-in-law for just a couple of weeks. The war started when he was there, and he was killed close to Lipawa. Abraham, though, opened a butcher's shop in Montevideo, took good care of his children. Then, fascists came to power. They disliked Jews and Jewish businesses, to put it mildly, so Abraham had to move to Israel.

Samuil was named after his maternal grandfather. At home they called him "Mulia." Nobody in his neighborhood made fun of this nickname because they simply wouldn't dare. In the neighborhood he was known as Senia or Sema. There were no strangers on their block and everybody knew each other.

Nobody ever helped Samuil, so he learned to deal with everything on his own. He liked taking care of himself, although he wasn't always successful. He dreamed of becoming a doctor, but who had time to think of that while working as a stevedore. If he didn't do it, who would?

He liked it in Voroshilovgrad. There was a river there called Luganka. Even though it wasn't good for swimming, it was still better than nothing. The city also boasted a museum dedicated to Voroshilov, who was often discussed in class.

Altogether, school was fun, and he was a good student, almost the best. From time to time, though, when classes got boring, he felt like screaming at the top of his lungs. God only knows how he managed to keep himself from doing it.

In elementary school and even later, teachers often made students black out textbook portraits of former leaders, which was cool. There were very few leaders left to cross out by the time Samuil reached grade six.

In summer, Samuil and his best friend Grishka would go to the river-bank or cycle. They had a special kind of whistle to call on each other. Samuil whistled really well. He could do a regular whistle, a wolf whistle, a pucker whistle. He knew how to whistle using two fingers and three, or even just one - the pinkie.

Samuil and Grishka cycled at full speed across streets, lanes, pavements, anything. The went so fast that chickens fled from under their wheels, hawk-like, while horses forgot to neigh and just hiccupped, sparks not just flied but fled from the wheels of their bicycles, and passers-by called them "yobs" or other, even more unfair and meaningless names.

Once, when Grishka was cycling in his usual unflappable high-speed manner, he ran into some stupid pebble and flipped Samuil over the wheel. Samuil ended up plowing with his nose the dust between hysterical geese and a half-dead, obese pig. He was hurt and miserable over the loss of the bicycle, and it was especially annoying to have all those onlookers gather around to stare at his mishap. Of course, he got over it eventually, he always did, but his nose remained a little crooked forever, even though it wasn't very noticeable. Actually, it was pretty hard to notice, to tell the truth.

They also loved it when it snowed really hard, the snowflakes crowding like soccer fans on their way to the stadium. While it snows, you can ski as fast as you can, screaming at the top of your lungs because here you can finally do it, and nobody can tell you to stop. Besides, there isn't anybody to tell because everybody is home, except Grishka and Samuil. Staying at home on a day like this, what can be sillier?

VIII

Vladimir Fedorovich and Klara were going to the zoo. They walked down the gubernatorial Sumskaya Street passing by the day care building and the endless Dzerzhinsky Square, by the Military Academy that proudly towered over everybody, by the pale yellow Engineering House where Maria worked and that looked like it was trying to soar over the square as a still sleepy morning sun. They walked by the solemn Gosprom sky-scraper, by the Pioneers' Palace and by Shevchenko's monument.

Vladimir Fedorovich held on to Klara's hand really hard because if you don't hold on to her you'll have a hard time catching up with her. He was wearing a white linen suit and a canotier hat. They walked slowly while Klara was telling him about the shocking discovery she had made before going out: the last Russian tsar Nicholas (the one Vladimir Fedorovich contemptuously referred to as Nikolashka) and a King of Great Britain (Edward or George) looked like two peas in a pod. Actually, they looked like a single pea. The only difference between them was that the king could be found on a stamp while the tsar was on a coin. Vladimir Fedorovich smiled while trying to steer the conversation towards Papanin's expedition. Klara, however, was as impossible to distract from her line of reasoning as Maria.

Vladimir Fedorovich, just hear this out," she prattled on. "They even have the same beard! I mean, beards. And moustaches. Everything is completely the same! How can that be?"

"Why are you so interested in their beards?" Vladimir Fedorovich smiled, looking joyfully at passers-by, proud of his erudite and sharp-eyed daughter.

"Hallo, Volodia! Hallo, Klarochka!" were they greeted by Zinovi. "What are you discussing that's so much fun?"

"Dad, get this, our tsars - ours and the British one - are probably the same person!" announced Klara her greatest, earth-shattering piece of news.

Zinovi kissed both of her dimpled cheeks and shook Vladimir Fedorovich's hand.

"What a child, this one!" smiled Vladimir Fedorovich smiled while lighting a cigarette he took out of an unusually-looking beautiful wooden box. "Since when are they ours, these guys? Tsar Nikolashka, may the devil take him, was overthrown, so to say, a long time ago."

"They don't have a tsar in Great Britain, they have a king," Zinovi added, partaking from Vladimir Fedorovich's beautiful box. "How are you getting on, Volodia? What's new?"

"We are on our way to the zoo, Zinovi," Vladimir Fedorovich said. "Maria is at work, so I took a day off. We were planning to go yesterday but the weather was bad."

"As for me, I like any kind of weather," Zinovi said. "I don't care what weather it is, as long as it is."

"I couldn't agree more, Zinovi," nodded Vladimir Fedorovich. "Still, it's better to walk to the zoo when it's dry than to trudge through the mud."

"That's true," Zinovi either sighed or inhaled the smoke, Klara couldn't tell. "But you and I both know that one day there will be no weather at all..."

He laughed and added, "So let it be any kind of weather!"

Vladimir Fedorovich nodded again. Zonovi shook his hand and kissed Klara.

"Dad, listen," Klara kept trying to convince him either to understand or to stay. "How can he be a king if he looks just like the tsar?"

Zinovi hugged her, winked at Vladimir Fedorovich, and offered a Solomonic decision,

"Honey, deep down inside every king wants to be a tsar while every tsar considers himself a king. You, however, are better than any princess or tsarevna. Isn't that so, Volodia?"

"Of course!" Vladimir Fedorovich confirmed. "Sometimes she misbehaves a little but princesses and tsarevnas should be allowed a little leeway there."

Zinovi smiled, waved good-bye and went in the direction that was opposite from theirs. Probably, he was going back to his place on Mayakovskaya Street.

IX

Klara and Vladimir Fedorovich were approaching the gates of the zoo when they saw a tiny little dog whom Klara took for a wind-up mouse looking like a tiny little dog. The mouse was dragging behind a corpulent lady who looked as proud and grandiose as the Salamander House on Sumskaya Street or even as Gosprom itself. The mouse was sniffing around on the sidewalk and in the grass next to it. Klara forgot all about the unexplained likeness between the two kings, or, rather, a king and a tsar, and began considering whether the mouse would succeed in dragging the lady to the bushes when something unexpected happened.

Another couple caught up with the lady and the mouse, consisting of a huge black dog wearing no muzzle ("It's a German shepherd," Vladimir Fedorovich explained while bending to Klara) and leading on a leather leash a lady with an intellectual look and an indistinct coloring similar to that of the German church on Pushkinskaya Street. This lady's figure reminded Klara of a yoke placed in an upright position. The three of them - the huge dog, the leather leash and the yoke - looked like an integral whole.

"A big black bug bit a big black dog on his big. . . " Klara quoted.

The more dogs Klara met, the clearer it became to her that dogs cannot be separated from their owners, even though people who said that dogs and their owners looked alike were wrong according to her observations. The king, as she suddenly remembered, truly looked like the tsar, while the mouse and the huge dog had nothing in common with their human companions. That was something to make one wonder.

At that point, the mouse noticed the huge German dog, opened her microscopic maw that hardly deserved the name it was so tiny, yelped and started squealing with such an abandon that Klara's hand that was being held by Vladimir Fedorovich got sweaty with fear. The mouse was jumping up, propelling itself into the air, trying to reach the huge dog and only getting as high as the ankle of the big lady holding her on a leash. "If only the mouse were wearing a white linen shirt," Klara mused, "it would have bravely torn it open on its chest." Although, there was as little chest on that dog as there were maw.

The huge dog paid no attention to the mouse's squealing and continued on her way without even straining the leash. The mouse, however, squealed with such desperation that the German dog decided to bring her out of her fit of hysteria. She turned around, uttered a thoughtful bark, and continued leading her owner on her way.

In response, the lions and the coyotes of the neighboring zoo recognized a familiar sound and howled in response. The crows let out their trademark nevermores. The trolleys on Sumskaya Street froze in their tracks.

". . . black nose," Klara finished the quote.

Seeing all the trouble she caused, the big dog sighed and led her lady friend away, still without even straining her leash ("to avoid stumbling over it," suggested Vladimir Fedorovich, who didn't look in the least scared.)

Klara recovered from her astonishment, raised her index finger and, in an attempt to calm herself down, announced: "This is what happens when you bark at an elephant."

In the meanwhile, the mouse's owner was trying to move her poor petrified animal. She tugged at the leash and urged her along. The mouse, however, was riveted to the spot, staring glassy-eyed into the translucent distance. Finally, the owner peeled her beloved pet off the ground with both hands and carried it away hugging and kissing it. At the spot where this occurred, where her petrified baby had just been sitting, a wet dime-sized patch remained.

"Don't be afraid," Vladimir Fedorovich said, patting Klara on the head. "Big dogs are smart, they don't bite kids. Tiny dogs might feel like biting but they have nothing to bite with."

He took a cigarette out of a pretty plastic or wooden box, which was more of a wondrous little container, and lit up. They went on to the zoo, while Klara kept thinking about different kinds of dogs, asking herself a question that didn't seem to have an answer: "They are both dogs, so why are they so dogged in their animosity?"

"Doggone!" she enunciated a funny new word, whose flow reminded her of a jumping rope or the tail of a large mouse. Then, she raised her hand and repeated it with a stress on the double 'g': "Doggone!"

Also, Klara remembered her favorite expression that Vladimir Fedorovich taught her when she was little and imagined a weeping cat whose tears constituted the wet spot under the tiny mousy dog.

Vladimir Fedorovich smiled and handed Klara an elongated round lollipop which was red, juicy and sweet. He glanced around to see whether passers-by noticed them: he was taking Klara to the zoo and was proud of his intelligent daughter.

X

When they came home from the zoo, Mom was home - she had just come back from her business trip to Leningrad. The door to the balcony was open, letting the aroma of their kneidlach soup waft over the entire Pushkin Entry. Nana Klara and Auntie Haya used to make this soup for them in Rechitsa. They also made great gefilte fish that had the aroma of Rechitsa and later Kharkov. It was a sight for sore eyes, and one felt reluctant to eat it until, having actually tried it, felt not only in seventh heaven but in seventeenth.

"How was the zoo?" Maria asked, interrupting Klara's internal monologue after Klara had washed her hands.

I didn't like the zoo at all because it was like a prison for animals. "Animal prison" would be a good name for it. Or you could say "Bestial jail", that would work even better. Just think about it: a huge grizzly bear - not a teddy-bear of children's tales, not a gummy bear, but a real-life grizzly - is pacing around as a prisoner of the Peter and Paul fortress, while little urchins who'd be better off locked up instead of him throw him candy and laugh at their own greatness and generosity. I can only imagine how they would laugh if the bear - not a gummy bear but this one, the real one - would have left his prison cell and asked them politely to swallow all this candy at once, wrappers and all.

"A penny for your thoughts," said Vladimir Fedorovich, smiling.

Maria observed,

"Volodia, don't you see that the child has become absent-minded? She is over-stimulated outdoors. Why not just stay at home, read a book? What possessed you to drag her to the zoo again?"

Vladimir Fedorovich shrugged his shoulders.

"If she keeps reading at the rate she does now, she will run out of books to read. Writers can't keep up. This way the child breathed fresh air for three hours."

"Fresh air in the zoo?" Maria protested. "Petkevich, why are you annoying me? Why are you forcing the child to breathe in all these elephants and camels?"

"It smells great in the zoo," Klara tried to stem the conflict and reassure her mother. In reality, the zoo didn't just smell, it did something even worse than that. To use a word she once heard from Vladimir Fedorovich, the picture would be as realistic as one by nineteenth-century painters: "Malodorousness." You have to raise your fingers and enunciate with gusto and with an understanding, stressing all three "o"s, especially the first one: "Mal-o-do-rousness."

"Neither Sumskaya nor Pushkinskaya Streets have anything like the smell of the zoo!" she assured her mother, thinking of malodorousness and hoping to calm Mom down and finish the last kneidlach in peace.

Vladimir Fedorovich laughed and added: "We also tried to figure out why our tsar Nikolashka was so similar to the British king. Imagine, Maria, Klara found a lot in common between them."

Maria gave Vladimir a terrifying look and offered her final verdict: "Petkevich, do you know why people have teeth? You think the teeth are for showing them? No, they exist so that one can keep one's tongue behind them."

"That's true," Vladimir Fedorovich agreed, still smiling out of habit. "Or somebody can knock them out. There is always someone who'd like to knock something out. And finding something to knock out is very easy."

"Be quiet, Petkevich!" Maria said to end the argument. "Or I will make you quiet. Just to think of it: "our" Nikolashka, indeed. Teaching something like this to a child. No more of that!"

With this she considered the discussion closed and, having calmed down a bit, addressed Klara in a strict voice as soon as she saw her get up from the table: "Here is a gift for you. Pushkin's poetry. It has just been published to mark the 100 anniversary of his death."

The book was thin, with coffee-colored covers that had mother-of-pearl undertones.

"No happiness exists, just force of will and peace," said a random line Klara noticed.

She kept repeating this line to herself as she went out into the balcony. Pushkin Entry was beneath her, thoughtful and mysterious as a line of poetry that had been read and repeated but had not become any clearer. Somebody invisible blew a gust of wind onto the poplars, and thousands of ethereal snow-white butterflies soared over Pushkin Entry and over the entire city of Kharkov.

Why doesn't it exist when it so obviously does? Here it is - soaring in weightless marshmallows, rustling the leaves of poplars, maples, chestnut-trees and oaks, reflecting sunbeams in the windows across the street...

So why would anybody say it doesn't exist?

Klara imagined another little girl, also named Klara, at the same time but not right now coming out into her courtyard in Rechitsa. That girl saw the same world, if only a little - just a tiny bit - different. Smoothed down her hair. The bright sun that looked like a bunny made her sneeze. She considered what she was going to do today, where her parents would take her, what they would discuss and with whom.

And... Well, how can one explain this, even to oneself? Now, right now, this girl does not exist but she used to. And nobody even considers that now, at this very moment but not right now, she is standing in the middle of her courtyard, smoothing her hair, thinking how she would pass the day, just not today. Here she is - can't you see her? - going into the house because her mother called her in. Here they go, all dressed up, because it is Saturday today. Here they are walking around Rechitsa. Here they are paying a visit to their friends. Sitting down to dinner. Talking, laughing, eating soup with kneidlach.

Here they are.

There they were.

Maybe this is why no happiness exists? Because what was now isn't, and those who were now aren't? Even though here they are...

Klara stood on the balcony and wasn't thinking about all this just yet. These thoughts simply flashed by, flew next to her like fluffy butterflies. Later, though, not often but every once in a while, they came back to her, always clearer than before, but there still was no answer. For a long time to come, there was none... How could she find an answer, if she didn't even know whether it existed? Is it possible that the answer always disappears together with those who once were but now are not?

Maybe happiness is that very answer that disappears with them?

The mother-of-pearl evening took the place of the day that floated away on the cloud of weightless marshmallows. Klara wasn't on the balcony facing Pushkin Entry anymore. And she didn't know that there would be a day when she would think that once she went out into the balcony and bits of poplar fluff that looked like ethereal butterflies were floating by her.

XI

In the summer of 1941, they had been evacuated for a couple of months, three months at most. My kings and queens ended up all alone for three whole years because nobody cared about them in the absence of their owner who had gone away with Maria Isaakovna and Vladimir Fedorovich. They were sent to a small town in the Ural Mountains called Hrompik. Kids nicknamed it Hrompupik, which sounded like a very small Hrompik.

Adults worked even more than they did before the war, they were hardly ever home. Getting home from work and then back would mean losing two whole hours, and there weren't enough hours in the day as it was.

Klara was as good of a student as back in Kharkov. There probably wasn't a better student than her in the entire Urals region. Her notebooks didn't have not only cross-outs (when did Stolberg ever have a cross-out?) but even a single typo. Just soft letters slightly bending to the left.

In the Urals Klara had the same Dnieper experiences that she thought had ended in Rechitsa. When she left for school, it would be even darker outside, and when she came back home it was dark as well. Time seemed to have stopped having meaning. The snow did not descend - the times of its condescension stayed in Kharkov. The snow didn't fall. Rather, it plunged down from the skies, screaming like a crazed cat, and this plunging continued the entire time she walked home from school and then again on her way back. Stockings had to be patched up constantly, especially on the knees, but everywhere else as well. Her felt boots didn't fulfill their purpose any longer. The snow that came both from the snow mounds and from the sky (if that scary mix could even be called a sky) got inside them. More than anything, she wanted to sit down in a snow mound and catch an uncatchable breath, but she knew that you can't stop. If you do, you might never come up for air any more. Just like Mary realized this when she first swam: to get where you need, you have to keep swimming.

To get where she needed Klara had to keep walking. She walked and recited passages from Pushkin's *Dubrovsky* and *The Captain's Daughter* that she had read dozens of times at Pushkin Entry. Or she would recite the multiplication table rhymes: "Two shoes kicked the door, two times two equals four. A tree on skates fell on the floor, three times eight is twenty-four. Skate, skate, figure eight's all the way to the shore, eight times eight is sixty-four."

She kept on walking while the snow screeched like a faulty dentist's drill and moaned like a patient whose teeth were being drilled. This unexpected comparison sounded hilarious to Klara and she would have certainly laughed if she'd managed to open her mouth. Then she had to unlock the door that had been frozen stuck and plastered over with snow like a tooth cavity. She didn't know what tooth fillings were made of but there was enough for her to think about other than tooth fillings, and each year she got more new ideas, and each one was more interesting than the previous ones.

By sheer miracle (of which there were so many) Klara managed to unlock the door of this communal flat, the first in her life. She put down the satchel (she didn't toss it or throw it, just put it down), changed her clothes, washed her face in the water that was cold even for the Urals, sat down, and got deep into thought, as usual. The main thing she thought about was that she had crossed her Dnieper and would now never sink.

Ahead of her - if only you looked very carefully - was her entire, as yet untouched life, the end of which she couldn't see. It was endless in spite of snow mounds and the screeching snow.

XI

Samuil was also walking but he wasn't going home from school or to school from home. He walked from the mill to the bakery and back along the endless ten-kilometer-long Arkul road, carrying a sack of flour on his back. They had been evacuated to Arkul from Voroshilovgrad: the parents, Semen Mikhailovich and Rosa Samoilovna, and the children, Samuil and his sister Ida with her baby daughter Maia.

During World War I, a German officer was quartered in Rosa's house. He was very polite and cultured, so you could see his good upbringing from the start. Those Germans were good people. They didn't organize pogroms and respected the people in whose houses they stayed. Everybody hoped that in this war the Germans would be as nice as the ones during the previous war, but things turned out to be very different, so they had to get evacuated.

Two months before the war started, on the day of Lenin's birthday, Samuil turned fifteen. In Arkul, he got a job at the mill, lugging flour sacks to the bakery. Arkul was a tiny little town, as small as Hrompik or Pervouralsk, but it was located on the Volga River, in Kirov region. There were very few non-conscripted men left. There were also no trucks. Semen Mikhailovich worked at the factory, and Samuil had to do the work of a grown man or a truck. He carried heavy flour sacks ten kilometers to the bakery and then walked back ten kilometers empty-handed to get a new flour sack. In this way he delivered two sacks a day.

He'd walk, carrying a sack on his back and thinking about how he walked on and on, and nobody got in his way - let them just try stopping him! - and that the padded jacket gave some warmth, even though it was a bit too wide for him, and the boots let almost no snow, rain or mud get in.

The sweat streamed down his face from under the hat or the cap as if it were an entire Luganka River. He had no way of wiping it off, but who cares about something like that.

He carried his sack and laughed out loud when he considered that some people got to carry on like fools while he got to carry flour sacks. When he stopped laughing, he sang songs or arias from his endless repertoire - in Russian, in Ukrainian, in Yiddish. The crows in the trees would fall silent in shame and listen to him jealously ready to eat crow in recognition that they were incapable of reproducing the Neapolitan melodies, the Jewish "Mama", "Eh, the roads" and "The night is starry" that Samuil performed in a tenor that was just about to break. They sat in the branches of a thousand trees, trying to look like life's lords and masters, but ended up reminding one of bits of November mud that had moved from the bare road to the bare tree branches. In winter, all these endless trees looked as useless as cigarette butts, but in summer they were as pleasantly disheveled as Samuil's head after a long working day (and night).

In Voroshilovgrad, Samuil attended a Ukrainian school, which is why he had two native languages. He recited poetry very well, especially "I saw a dream so strange" in Ukrainian. He also knew Yiddish because his parents spoke it to each other and to the kids. His mother also liked singing Jewish songs. Gradually, though, they learned to speak Russian as well.

Before Arkul, Samuil had never really fallen in love but now he fell in love with a woman twice his age. If Semen

Mikhailovich hadn't gotten involved, things would have been very different, even though at that time Samuil couldn't imagine just how different. Semen Mikhailovich did get involved, though, and when Kharkov was liberated and they were allowed to return, the family went straight there.

As for Grishka, he must have remained in the place he'd been evacuated to, and then moved to another town because he wasn't in Voroshilovgrad any more. And later on, he wasn't in Lugansk either.

Samuil walked along the same road to pick up the second sack of the day. His hands were in the pockets of his padded jacket. He wished he hadn't run out of cigarettes but who cares anyways? Bits of mud were leaping from underneath his boots like the chickens had leapt from under the wheels of his bicycle in Voroshilovgrad or like sparks under the hooves of a Voroshilovgradian horse. Branches stuck out of the trees like spokes out of the wheels of that same bicycle after it got broken. He was walking to get his second sack of the day, singing in an almost formed tenor or reciting a Voroshilovgradian rhyme: "Anna vanna, tantania, sia via campania. Salamadaraki tiki-taki, sie vie van."

Ahead of him an endless life stretched on which couldn't be obscured even by the stupid mill with all of its flour and all of its sacks.

It was endless because how can such a great life possibly end, if everything depends only on myself, and everything will be just the way I planned.

XII

The war wasn't over yet, but Kharkov had been liberated from the Nazis, so Maria Isaakovna decided to go back to Kharkov. She had been offered an important job in Ufa, but Kharkov was Kharkov, and no other city was a match for it. It was more fun working in Kharkov because all engineers and scholars in her discipline were there, as well as university and college professors. Of course, it was also her second motherland.

They settled down in a communal apartment on Sumskaya Street, close to Dzerzhinsky Square, ten minutes away from Shevchenko Gardens. It took about the same time to reach the Gorky Park if you took a trolley. Their apartment at Pushkin Entry had been occupied, and they hadn't been allowed back in. The people who took over their flat didn't give back the stamps with the kings and the queens, let alone silver rubles and the white baby grand piano.

Maria Isaakovna got a job at the imposing Engineering House which was located at the Dzerzhinsky Square, right next to the Gosprom. Vladimir Fedorovich was working at a job that was similar to the one he had in the Urals. He started working at the Southern Railway Bureau that was located at the imposing Kharkov Railway Square.

Klara's Kharkov world grew in size. Her walk back home from school was now longer than before the war but it was also more fun. She still attended the same prestigious school in a quiet downtown area. They lived on the majestic Sumskaya

Street, on the fourth floor of a tall and bulky seven-floor building that had been built during the reign of Alexander the Second or the Third.

Pushkinskaya Street had tram rails and looked like an attractive intellectual student from a college for noble young ladies who found its place easily in the twentieth century. Sumskaya Street, on the other hand, reminded one of Ellen Besukhova from Tolstoy's *War and Peace*. Every once in a while it also looked like Catherine the Great because it was curvaceous, luxuriant, and a little funny in its majestic and irrepressible pride. Walking down Pushkinskaya Street she felt like melting of love for somebody yet unknown and saw herself as a cloud in a dress (to use poet Mayakovsky's metaphor), reciting almost out loud thousands of books she had read or was going to read.

On Sumskaya Street, under the unrelenting gaze of the monument immortalizing the poet Taras Shevchenko, she couldn't stop herself from admiring it. Then, she could walk into the oldest and consequently the most impressive grocery store and buy fifty grams of her favorite smoked sausage. She couldn't do that now, of course, but after the war was over, she definitely would.

Pushkinskaya Street was for sauntering because there was no reason to hurry on a street like this one. It was for thinking vague though mysteriously profound and deep thoughts that couldn't be shared with anybody else.

Sumskaya was not for thinking. It was reserved for smiling at the happy realization that the war would soon be over, for breathing in the trolley smell, for breathless admiration of its beloved condescending buildings. She used to walk in Shevchenko Gardens, gathering split chestnuts and prying shiny glistening cores out of them. They looked like they had been washed in the Lopan River before being stuck inside the chestnuts and hung on the trees.

Pushkinskaya looked like a dreamy chestnut alley in Shevchenko Gardens, while Sumskaya was like Pushkinskaya that was all grown up. Sumskaya and Pushkinskaya never crossed paths. They ran alongside each other like the earth and the skies. For this very reason, they couldn't be imagined without each other, like the back and the front of one palm.

Kharkov also couldn't be imagined without these two streets. Is there ever a palm without the front and the back?

XIII

At first, Samuil didn't have to go anywhere. He lived with his parents, Ida and Maia, almost at the end of the world - in the Balashovka area, on a tiny Dobrokhotov Street. It was as quiet there is in an empty fish-tank. They had a small courtyard with dahlias and some other strange rose-petalled and long-stemmed flowers. When he walked down the street, the dust would rise up but not in a cloud as it said in books. Books were always wrong and reading them was a drag. If he had to compare the dust to something he would say it looked like an old, dirty, darned blanket. He'd walk down the street, sneeze, and wonder why he even needed this stupid Balashovka, these old-fashioned houses with their courtyards, the railway station with cargo trains, wobbly benches and dirty window-sills.

I'd like for things to be different. I want to become a doctor and in my hospital - or, rather, in my clinic - there wouldn't be a single speck of dust, let alone an entire cloud of it. Doctors, nurses and paramedics will wear white coats that will be starched to the point where they will be as crunchy as the pre-war chocolate wrapper. The window-panes will be so clean that you will hardly be able to see them. In the waiting room, there will be comfortable couches which might even have cushions if people feel like it. Bathrooms will have tiled walls. There will also be a library, a playroom, and a canteen that will be no worse than any pre-war restaurant. In the canteen it will smell not of stale borscht but of fresh vegetable soup and fried pre-war potatoes.

Soon the war will be over and everything will be just like I planned: the tiles, the couches, the vegetable soup. Then I will be able to go to medical school and then finally don this magical white coat with bluish undertones, put a stethoscope around my neck and ask an old lady whose fingers are crooked because of old age and constant field labor, "What is your complaint, patient?" And then I'll cure her, and her fingers - in spite of what some know-it-alls might expect - will straighten out.

Then I'll take to task an obese gentleman whose heavy breathing prevents every patient in his ward from falling asleep, "If you, my dear sir, don't start taking physical exercise, your heart muscle will turn into a threadbare dishcloth. Or even into a dirty facial tissue."

And if the director of the clinic asks me, "Samuil Semenovich, are you sure you are not being too harsh?", I will respond to this older but not necessarily more experienced colleague of mine that the best way to help is by being respectful but firm.

The obese patient will start taking care of himself. He will exercise, shed a lot of weight and many of his worries and will free up the space in the ward to a new patient. Whom Samuil will obviously cure as well.

When Samuil turned eighteen, he went to a vocational school to train as a fitter. There was nothing for him to do at his parents' house in Balashovka. He was permanently hungry but there was nothing to eat. It was even worse than in Arkul. Samuil kept growing, and his height made it even more obvious how skinny he was. Lugging flour sacks had kept him fit in the same way that athletes stayed fit as a result of regular cross-country races. So he decided to get trained for a blue-collar profession first. It could always come in handy, especially if at first he didn't manage to get accepted to the medical school. One day he would be able to go to that unattainable med school where so many people applied that it was next to impossible to get in.

Well, it might have been impossible for other people to get in. Samuil, however, was the kind of person who could carry a flour sack from the mill to the bakery in all kinds of weather and during any time of the day or the night. The harder it was for him to carry the sack, the louder he sang his Neapolitan songs. He noticed neither the endless road nor his own arms and legs that were completely numb nor the sack. He knew that his heart would be able to withstand everything and never turn into a threadbare dishcloth or a dirty facial tissue.

At the vocational school, Samuil was one of the best students. He lived in the school's dorm. He had a single pair of pants but they had the kind of flare that stopped women of all age groups and social classes in their tracks. Fellow students from their vocational school would get together in their dorm room and sang songs. When Samuil reached for the highest Neapolitan note and made it last forever and longer, all floors of the dorm heard him and listened to him. Even the people in neighboring houses and possibly even the passengers of the passing vehicles must have heard him. You can't really say that he was the life of the party because this would have meant that the party was bigger than him and that he was just a small part of it. In reality, he was the party and there would have been no party if he hadn't been there. Of course, it's possible that this is exactly what it means to be the life of the party.

XIV

Their privileged school was located in the quiet downtown area which was considered Kharkov's best neighborhood. Klara was the stellar student there. Theirs was a select group of students, even though nobody had selected them on purpose. You couldn't say that other girls in the group were worse students than Klara. They weren't worse, it was simply that she was better. For Klara, the thirteen final exams that awaited them, even the geometry final that made everybody shudder in terror, were easier than a piece of cake. They were more of an air-light eclair for her. In her notebooks one wouldn't find not only cross-outs (Klara Stolberg and cross-outs couldn't have been brought together even by Jules Verne's imagination) but even a single typo that would have allowed a stranger to heave a sigh of relief. Just soft letters slightly bending to the left that looked as if somebody restrained horses that had been moving at a full gallop.

One time only did the fat lady sing for Klara, and that lady wasn't fat at all. She was a perennially fifty-something teacher of the Russian language and literature, a refined aristocrat in a hopelessly armored dress and a pince-nez that precluded any thought that relationships might be easy. Her name was Elena Filippovna Raiskaya. Before the revolution, she had attended a school for noble ladies and was obviously and exclusively a noble lady.

For this reason, her students referred to her as a Rose-Fingered Maiden. The Rose-Fingered Maiden's demeanor was so strict and her gaze behind the pince-nez was so sharp that they could only be compared with the strictness and the sharpness of everybody's silently beloved geometry. The teacher was also generally beloved, although that was also done quietly.

"Language," she used to say, "isn't just the matter of 'what?' but also a matter of 'how?' and both 'what?' and 'how?' are equally significant. This is why we will study both of them equally."

Well, on the day when the aforementioned fat lady delivered her performance, the teacher called on Klara to answer a question on Mayakovsky whom Klara, together with Stalin, did not mind acknowledging as the best and the most talented poet of the century.

"Stolberg," said the Rose-Fingered Maiden with a secret sense of repressed enjoyment while rolling her "r"s as proof of her self-evident parentage. "Please come to the blackboard."

The best student stepped forward, patted down her black pinafore that she wore over a brown dress and started talking about Mayakovsky's play "Bedbug". While she was speaking, she couldn't stop thinking about a comedy she had seen at the Zhdanov movie theater the day before with one of her numerous admirers. Then, all of a sudden, she surprised herself - let alone the rest of the students - but herself still even more by saying, to the point but in a linguistically atrocious way: "Irregardless."

The rose petals were torn off the rose by a gust of wind, the nightingale choked up and fell silent, and the thorns shrank. For a moment, the Rose-Fingered Maiden looked like a wilted rosebud. She felt degraded, demeaned and debased in the midst of performing the sacred duty of teaching. In indignation, she raised her pince-nez with trembling fingers and regaled Klara with a terrifying glare. Then she enunciated while rolling her "r"s in the same way as Marshal Ney must have done as he was confronting Kutuzov at Borodino in 1812,

"Stolbegg!?.."

Or maybe it even sounded more like:

"Stolbehg!?.."

"And also," Klara continued, while her face grew purple to reflect her emotional state, but never skipping a beat, "he would say, 'I ain't got nothing to object.' A great writer always creates a character who reflects his origins."

"What on Earth do you have against Mayakovsky's origins?" the Rose-Fingered Maiden inquired all atremble.

"I'm talking about the character," Klara responded proudly while the blush covered her cheeks right above her dimples.

She felt like a military leader who lost the battle but won the war.

XV

The spring of 1945 was even more luxurious than what springs used to be like before the war. It started on March 8, the International Women's Day, when almost all of the male students greeted Klara. The number of dark-haired, fair, red-headed, short, tall, skinny and fat guys who were in love with her made Klara laugh. They all blushed, stammered and went pale while trying to keep their trembling gaze on her blush and her dimples, let alone on any other part of her body (let them only try!)

Their adoration was slightly pleasing to her but not necessary. Equally unimportant was the first and for now the last kiss that she had engineered in seventh grade for purposes of reconnaissance and acquiring a basic kind of experience. The only man she found attractive was Marshal Rokossovsky. Klara knew her own worth, so all these symbolic trophies that were being laid at her feet brought her no new information. Klara knew that she wasn't simply beautiful. That was what her post-war friend Mila was. Overall, there was no shortage of beautiful women. As for Klara, she knew that her beauty was unique, in a way that never really happens. When it does happen it is not even an exception to the rule. It's a completely opposite rule altogether.

Her features, smile, facial expressions, gait and everything else did not belong to any ethnic group. Rather, they were a heady mix of several. Her appearance was the result of centuries-long inhuman effort. This complex project started in the Holy Land and continued in the Pyrenees. After Columbus's voyage, it developed in several different kingdoms and tsardoms and culminated in Kharkov where the Demiurge must have wiped the sweat off his forehead and said with a heavy sigh, "That's it, I can't do any better." He was being modest, of course. The project was completed not because the author had grown tired but simply because he had achieved his goal.

Men fell in love with Klara even more often than with Maria. All of the people who were hopelessly in love with her (which in itself is a tautology because who else was there to fall in love with hopelessly?) felt towards her a kind of a hopeless fear that was closer to awe. These hopeless suitors knew that there were no books in existence that she hadn't read. And even if such books were to appear, she would eventually read them. And if she didn't, that would simply mean that they didn't deserve her attention. There were no questions she couldn't answer. Of course, she knew well enough that such questions existed and there were quite a few of them, but these were questions of the kind that she could only answer for herself. People around her hardly even knew that these questions existed, let alone had answers to them.

Her regard was too precious to be deserved with something trivial like getting flustered, expressing one's feelings, looking at her with silent adoration, or serenading her (which nobody had yet thought of, but who knows what people might be capable of?) in a raspy voice under her balcony on Sumskaya Street. It would have been a pretty kettle of fish if somebody attempted to get in the way of her doing her homework, reading, learning English or listening to music in such a way.

Klara was quite sociable but while she was socializing with people and allowing them to socialize with her, she was unwittingly creating a transparent and at the same time impenetrable bubble that surrounded her and separated her from others. She wasn't doing it on purpose. Rather, her perennially terrified admirers did it for her. It was their own fault, of course, because Klara never asked them to fear her comments and think that she was making fun of people who made fools of themselves. She wasn't laughing at them (like she cared enough for that) but simply because she felt like laughing.

To give an example, Marik Steinberg, one of the top students in the entire city of Kharkov who was slated to receive a gold medal for his outstanding grades, fell in love with Klara to the point of stuttering. Of course, it is quite possible that he always stuttered, who knows? Finally, he decided to inform Klara of his feelings that were evident not only to her but to everybody else within a hundred mile radius. She burst out in a bout of compassionate (yes, compassionate, why can't anybody understand that?) laughter so that her blush turned from pale-pink to aggressively red. In a similarly compassionate tone that suggested she only wanted the best for Marik, she responded, "Marik, have you ever seen yourself in the mirror?"

"Sure I have," Marik responded. His face was covered with huge beads of sweat that looked like boils.

Klara stopped laughing, looked at him seriously, and concluded, "In that case, your actions are incomprehensible."

She had nothing else to say, nor did she want to.

Maria Isaakovna respected the Steinberg family and thought that Marik would grow into somebody important, probably a famous doctor. She tried asking him over a few times, but Klara opposed her efforts because she realized that letting the poor love-stricken guy down would be harder than building his hopes up.

"I have no idea what more you want, child," Maria Isaakovna said. "He is a wonderful young man from a very good family."

"Mother," Klara responded once and for all, "I see nothing in him, including anything wonderful. As for his family, I'm quite content with mine."

Here Vladimir Fedorovich smiled knowingly but pretended that he was engrossed by his newspaper.

XVI

Marik was left alone with the scent of her perfume that always lingered in her wake without ever quite disappearing. Klara, in the meanwhile, was walking back to Sumskaya Street.

Around her – not just in Kharkov but probably all over the world that hadn't yet cured itself from the damage caused by war – spring was raging, raving and going crazy over its own beauty. This long-awaited month of April was bringing her closer to a red-letter day the likes of which the world had not yet seen and which made New Year's, the anniversary of the October Revolution and the International Workers' Day (the most important holidays the country celebrated) pale in comparison. This spring augured love that would cocoon her in quotes from the Romantic poet Tyutchev, throw the shadow of the Neuhausen castle over her, surround her with images from Turgenev's *Springtime Waters* or Musorgsky's *Pictures at an Exhibition*.

The snow that smelled like fresh milk stopped and trembled with laughter together with her and then flowed down Lermontovskaya Street, Pushkinskaya, Mayakovskaya, her entire city of Kharkov that winked at her with every window pane of every building on Chernyshevskaya, Karazinskaya, Sumskaya, Sovnarkomovskaya, Rymarskaya Streets.

While she walked, she composed poetry and music that might have been composed by somebody else already. This did not make them any less valuable to her, just the opposite.

She walked down Rymarskaya Street composing music and poetry when she suddenly caught a glimpse of a tall, extremely skinny guy whose black hair was combed back in the manner of the famous writer Nikolai Ostrovsky and whose eyes reflected sunbeams – imagine that! – coming from the windows of the opera house. It was also possible that his eyes were the source of the sunbeams, which was why he looked like a sunbeam himself.

The guy was going in the opposite direction, towards the Seminary Hill, in the company of similar but at the same time very different friends. It seemed that if somebody removed him from the group, everybody else would disappear too because without him this entire group – or posse, like some people would call it – will fall apart and lose all meaning. He was what made the group mean something because sunbeams were reflected in nobody else's eyes. Nobody else could make the sunbeams jump out and scatter around after reflecting them.

The guy was telling his friends something extremely funny in a voice of an opera singer at rest. They were falling over and gasping with laughter, slapping him on the shoulder, and then going back to falling over and gasping. The guy who looked like a sunbeam kept entertaining them. He laughed in a tenor that was similar to that of the famous opera singer Lemeshev and rolled a cigarette around in his mouth. He was wearing impossibly flared pants and a tattered jacket. His fingers were as long as a pianist's or possibly a surgeon's. Klara managed to notice nothing else because she wasn't staring all that hard or listening very attentively.

For Samuil this was the last time ever that he didn't notice Klara. His schoolmates and he had decided to take a walk downtown, have a beer, celebrate getting their stipends on that day. He was telling old Arkul and Kharkov jokes that crunched under his teeth like pickles fresh from a barrel.

Samuil loved walking on Rymarskaya Street, going down the Seminary Hill towards the enormous Blagoveschensky marketplace that always teemed with people and that was located close to the majestically quiet Blagoveschensky Cathedral. People said that the Seminary Hill had been named this way because during the tsar's times there was a seminary at the top of the hill, next to Sumskaya Street. During breaks between classes, students of the seminary would run down the hill like they were possessed, screaming "St. Jacob be with us!" They say that St. Jacob was considered the patron of Kharkov Seminary which is why the students brought him up whenever they had a chance. Market vendors were terrified of these St. Jacobians who would run into the marketplace with eyes flashing and almost foaming at the mouth, run between the stalls, grab everything in sight – and there was hardly anything that escaped being in their sight – and wreak a devastation that was similar to that of an actual pogrom.

Vendors called the St. Jacobians "syavkas", which was why Kharkov was the only place that had such a phenomenon. Of course, syavkas existed in other places too but they were called differently. Well, a syavka is a syavka, no matter what you call him. Then again, sometimes a guy is a total syavka but if you call him a name that's more decent, he'll still be a syavka though to a lesser degree. Say what you want, a lot depends on a name. And when nothing else is available, then everything depends on it.

Blagoveschensky Cathedral was quiet, otherworldly and grim during Easter. The air smelled of something churchy, possibly myrrh. The priest didn't look very impressive and the altar boys that either helped or served him seemed like they were there just to fill the space rather than to do something worthwhile.

What Samuil really liked were the holy images. Some of them looked like real paintings. Of course, it wasn't for nothing that they'd been painted by Repin himself. Who could have thought that this guy who lived in Chuguyev, a town just like Arkul that was a hundred times smaller than Kharkov and altogether impossible to compare to it, would decorate this big city with his paintings? Well, he didn't decorate the entire city, of course, just the cathedral. It was quite a big deal, though, to decorate Kharkov's main cathedral. It meant that one could do anything if one really tried.

Mary was especially stunning. As he looked at her, Samuil realized that this was the only woman who could have given birth to Jesus. Nobody else could have done it.

He lit a candle on the flame of one that was already burning, put it into a copper plate, pressing on it to ensure that it wouldn't fall over by accident. He wanted to cross himself but felt too shy. What's the point of making the sign of the cross with all those people around, anyway? When there are so many people all over the place, one is better off thinking, crossing himself by means of his thoughts rather than with his hand, and winking at a tranquil beauty on a painting by Repin.

People kept falling onto their knees and beating their foreheads against the floor. Still, if you get on your knees, it looks like you and she are not even friends, as if she is the person who gives you the orders to lug several heavy floursacks tomorrow. When, however, you wink at her, it feels like she winked at you too and you are good buddies. And it seems like she is telling you, "Look, try not to disappear for too long, OK? Come by whenever you feel like it. I'll be looking out for you."

He would straighten out the candle to make sure it wasn't falling over, smile imperceptibly and leave. . .

This kind of conversation took place on Easter and sometimes on New Year's Eve. However, on the day when Samuil failed to notice Klara for the first and for the last time in his life, he was walking down Rymarskaya Street with his school mates, passing the cherry-red like an old shawl building of the pawn house, descending the sky-high stairs next to the hill where the university was located. There, not far from the Southern railway station, right next to the place where the sixth tram route stopped and in front of the firefighters' precinct, there was a bar that reeked of smoke and that they could sometimes afford to patronize. This usually happened on the days when they received their stipends, and this was precisely one of those days.

Some people who had excessively strict views on life referred to them in the same way as the old-time vendors referred to the students of the seminary. This, however, was unfair because Samuil and his friends neither yelled nor grabbed stuff that was on sale. They just roared with laughter when they heard funny stories and jokes that Samuil told them. Or, to be precise, he didn't tell his funny stories, he enacted them, and those stories crunched on his teeth like pre-war pickles that came straight from the barrel.

XVII

Vladimir Fedorovich was walking down Trinkler Street, trying to avoid filling his shoes with icy water from puddles of melted snow and thinking that name changes, may the devil take them, were something he could neither understand nor accept. If something has a name, what's the point of changing it? And what does it mean to change a name if it already exists? In this manner, one could try renaming even Klara or Maria. This thought made him smile. People must have had something in mind when they originally named things.

Of course, it also happens that those who have something in mind are not the ones who engage in name changing. One could accept the change from German Street into Pushkinskaya Street that was done many years ago. Such a change made sense because who needs to name streets after Germans, anyway? All that was left from the old name on Pushkinskaya Street was a single German church, long and skinny like a true German woman. She reminded me of my old school-teacher. Of course, if one were to think about it, he would have never learned to write so well without that teacher, adding one letter to another carefully and slowly. He also wouldn't have learned to do his sums quite as well. He never got rid of his Polish accent though that could still be heard in the way he pronounced his "l"s. And neither did his sister Nadia. . .

All that was fine and well, but why would anybody have a problem with St. Nicholas Square? Well, obviously it got in the way of those who had had the brilliant idea to demolish St. Nicholas's Cathedral that was located right between Pushkinskaya Street and St. Nicholas Square. That square had carried the name of St. Nicholas forever but now it was called Tevelev. It was clear that the square hadn't been named to honor that silly Tsar Nicholas II because he hardly had any honor, may the devil take him. It must have been named after some saint or somebody like that. In any case, naming places after saints is better than naming them after God knows whom. I think nobody will rename a square to honor a decent person. Vladimir Fedorovich smiled once again without saying this out loud, of course.

Or let's take Pavel Square, for example. It is also located downtown, a little way down from St. Nicholas Square. It is actually very easy to get from there to the area where his sister Nadia lives or to take the eleventh tram route to the Southern railway station where he often goes to meet Maria when she returns from her business trips. So who had the brilliant idea to rename such an important square from Pavel to, God help us all, Rosa Luxemburg's Square? Was it done to make people twist their tongues trying to pronounce it? What does it even matter anymore who had given his name to this square? It might have been an emperor or yet another saint, but Pavel Square sounded easy to understand, pronounce and get used to, while Rosa Luxemburg's Square wasn't a real name but a political slogan.

It was a good thing that nobody had thought of renaming Sumskaya Street into some atrocity of the "Street of the Twenty-Six (or Seven) Commissaries from Baku" kind, like happened in many other cities. It made him smile just to imagine such a possibility.

And how about the military academy? This heavy edifice that seemed to breathe on the corner of Dzerzhinsky Square and Lenin Avenue was supposed to house the Ukrainian government. But then somebody who should better remain unnamed had the brilliant idea to move the capital from Kharkov to Kiev. Why Kiev and not Zhmerinka or Kozelschina, one might ask? Well, one didn't ask, of course, just thought to oneself, but still?

Vladimir Fedorovich shook his head and took a cigarette out of his magical wooden box. Maria didn't allow him to smoke. She always scolded him for his habit, called him an ashtray or even a cigarette butt. This usually made him smile and say, "Oh, for Pete's sake!" He kept his smoking secret from Maria. Klara knew that Vladimir Fedorovich smoked but kept his secret. He was grateful to her for that and appreciated her even more.

He was sorry that she had grown up. Well, not sorry, of course, just a little sad that there wasn't anybody he could take by the hand and take to the zoo anymore, so he had to spend a lot of time alone. As usual, he worked a lot. He had always been an ideal employee. He'd often bring his work home and sit there alongside Klara, each at their own desk. Klara would write her homework assignments in a soft handwriting with a slight leftwards slant. In the meanwhile, he'd fill out his graph sheets spread around the dinner table with letters that stood straight, without the slightest slant in any direction and without a single cross-out (Petkevich and cross-outs?). He'd also make calculations using an abacus and record the results in countless huge notebooks. Klara reckoned that Vladimir Fedorovich must have had several thousand documents. Still, each of them had its own pile, and each pile was in its own file, and each file had its own place in the bookcase. This is why he never had to look for things. Who needs to look where everything has its own, one and only, place?

Klara also enjoyed this almost supernatural order because she had realized how useful it was when she had first started staying home alone. Let's take a person's mouth, for example. It's not like you have to search for it when you bring a glass of lemonade or a piece of sausage up to it, right? The mouth is always there and nobody needs to look for it. Now let's imagine that you drank your lemonade and ate your sausage and then stuck your mouth in some obscure place. Then, the next time you needed it, you'd really have to sweat, and there is no guarantee that you'd even be able to locate your mouth and have a place to put your food and drink.

As he was thinking about all this, Vladimir Fedorovich crossed onto Girshman Street, then continued down Sumskaya and stood in front of their building for a while finishing his cigarette. Then, he located the wooden box with a slide-out cover, made sure that he hadn't misplaced it by mistake, put a fragrant piece of candy in his mouth and entered their imposing building that bore the number eighty-two.

XVIII

Maria was pleasantly appalled.

"Imagine this, Volodia," she was saying while placing the teacups and the saucers that Klara had washed and dried into the cupboard where they joined seven diminutive marble elephants that were ranged according to their size. "Kleiman tried complimenting me in a very clumsy manner today."

Klara was put on guard by this statement but didn't let it show. As usual, she gave the marble elephants a look and got behind her desk to do homework. She really liked the elephants, especially the biggest and the smallest ones. In the meanwhile, Maria Isaakovna continued,

"I was making a presentation about my project at the meeting of engineers, and Kleiman found nothing better to do than to announce in front of everybody that I had a male brain. Can you believe this?"

Vladimir Fedorovich was sitting in an armchair, in his favorite leather jacket with rabbit fur which was among the things they had received at the Urals as part of the lend-lease program. He was reading "Izvestiya." In response to Maria Isaakovna's question, he offered a tenuous smile, said "may the devil take this Kleiman" and turned over the page. Deep down he believed that distinguishing male brains from female ones was quite a boring occupation. Klara, however, remarked without interrupting her work on an essay about the temperamental Natasha Rostova whose reputation as a romantic heroine was contradicted by her tendency to embarrass Prince Andrei,

"If you cut something off of a male brain, you'll come up with a female one."

Vladimir Fedorovich giggled in a way that signaled either embarrassment or relief and hid behind a funny article in the newspaper he was reading. Maria Isaakovna exclaimed,

"Klara, who taught you to say things like these?"

"Or," Klara continued coldly while continuing her work on the essay, "you can sew the part you have cut off onto the female brain to create another male brain. People like Natasha Rostova and Kleiman consider this difference to be significant, while you and I do not. Sometimes, this difference is bigger, sometimes it's smaller. At other times, it is next to non-existent. Some people are deeply impressed with it, while others are left indifferent by it. I, for one, feel indifferent towards it in the best sense of the word. But only in the best sense, so there is no need to worry.

Maria Isaakovna was stunned both by the way Klara simplified the problem (or maybe made it more complex) and the extent of her knowledge in the matter. She also wondered about the source of such nontrivial information. It seemed to Klara as if the medals on the snow-white plaster bust that stood on the bookcase surveying the surroundings clinked to signal their support.

"Why are you laughing, Petkevich?" Maria Isaakovna raised her brows in indignation.

"Oh my God," Vladimir Fedorovich raised the hand that was free from holding the newspaper. "Should I now start crying because of your Kleiman?"

"What does Kleiman have to do with any of it? Have you heard what the child is saying? Then why don't you say a word? Do you have a word to say, Petkevich? It seems like when nobody needs them, you have a thousand words to say.

The moment they are needed, though, you are just sitting there, reading your paper."

"And that's how it always is," Vladimir Fedorovich smiled. "Your Kleiman, may the devil take him, always messes up, and I get blamed for that."

XIX

Maria didn't get the time to debate the point because their communal apartment was pierced with an inhuman scream, "Rape!!"

Maria Isaakovna's heart sank in a way it hadn't since the war had started on June twenty-second 1941. Vladimir Fedorovich dropped his newspaper, while Klara made an ink stain in her notebook (Stolberg and an ink stain?) between Natasha and Prince Andrei. What was really strange is that this did not upset her in the least. She ran to the door and looked out into the hallway in order to determine whether somebody was, indeed, getting raped, and if so, then who that was and how far the things had gone.

They shared their communal apartment with four other people: Strelkina, Volkova, Pipa, and the Feldmans. Only the Feldmans, Fira Markovna and Daniil Savvich, were nice people while the rest, as Vladimir Fedorovich used to say, were completely useless. In terms of appearance, Maria Isaakovna would mention that each of their neighbors looked scarier than a bombing raid. Klara had been lucky in that she never got to see bombing raids. Still, she found it hard to believe that anybody or anything could be scarier. From time to time, she would try to range her unpleasant neighbors according to the degree of their unpleasantness, but this exercise always ended in a draw.

Strelkina was in the habit of locking herself in what Vladimir Fedorovich referred to as the bathroom facilities and remain there for forty minutes each morning. Since the bathroom was communal, this meant that the neighbors could neither wash themselves nor do the opposite (in Klara's words). All efforts to get Strelkina to cease and desist failed utterly. Vladimir Fedorovich and Feldman turned to the authorities on various occasions, but that didn't work. Strelkina would arrive in the bathroom before anybody else could get there, lock herself inside for forty minutes (Vladimir Fedorovich referred to this state of affairs as a constipation), while everybody else, especially Klara and the inhabitants of the apartment who had to go to work (Maria Isaakovna, Vladimir Fedorovich and the Feldmans) were forced to put up with the deprivation.

Volkova, as Maria Isaakovna would say, did nasty things in secret. She was in the habit of leaving her garbage in front of her neighbors' doors. The worst part was that nobody could ever predict whose door she would choose each time to dispose of her garbage. "Volkova should be watched over," Vladimir Fedorovich woud say.

"And sniffed after," Klara would suggest.

As for Pipa, she was mysterious and unpredictable. When Maria Isaakovna, Vladimir Fedorovich and Klara had returned from the evacuation and came to live in this communal apartment number seven in the majestic building number eighty-two on the haughty and distracted Sumskaya Street, Klara tried to figure out what Pipa's full name would be. Penelope didn't sound right, and neither did Agrippina. Then, it turned out that "Pipa" was the woman's last name. Even so, this last name was quite mysterious. It wasn't a diminutive from a longer last name, such as, for example, Pipina, Pipman, Piptyuk or even Pipidze. Pipa was Pipa and not even Vladimir Fedorovich, who seemed to know everything there was to know about the communal apartment, could figure out what her first name was.

So while all neighbors knew that no matter when they were to get up in the morning, Strelkina would always be occupying the bathroom and Volkova would always manage to leave her garbage next to somebody's door no matter how hard people tried to watch over her or sniff after her, Pipa's actions remained impossible to fathom. She was capable of any kind of extravagant behavior, from purposefully over salting somebody else's borsch that was left on the communal stove to smearing the floors in the communal hallway with a foul-smelling brownish substance. At the same time, Pipa never repeated a single one of her weird actions twice. One easily got bored in her absence, and even a phlegmatic Strelkina who was one hundred percent committed to her personal physiology and a craftily ruthless Volkova would miss her. Pipa managed to entertain all and sundry.

To resume the story, when Klara heard what was either an enraged scream or a call to arms and sounded like "Rape!!", she ran into the communal hallway. Screams and shouts were coming from the direction of the communal kitchen. It was now clear that Pipa was the one screaming rape.

"What a thing to announce so loudly," Klara thought because Pipa's screams didn't sound much like a plea for help. When she stormed into the kitchen, Klara saw a scene that, to use an expression common to the kind of novels that she hadn't read for a while, made her blood run cold.

XIX

Vladimir Fedorovich threw off the newspaper with a gesture he had learned from the famous football player Privalov and ran after Klara. As he was running, he tried to keep his slippers from slipping off his feet. His goal was to be the first one to reach the communal kitchen in order to get between Klara and any danger that could have been awaiting her. Maria Isaakovna followed them. She knew well enough that without her they wouldn't be able to do anything right, which is why she was in no hurry.

A little while ago, Vladimir Fedorovich had experienced a similar kind of terror. The only difference was that Klara had been in no danger on that occasion. After finishing work, Vladimir Fedorovich arrived at a colleague's apartment at the exact time they had agreed on (Petkevich being late?). The colleague had an apartment of his own, one he didn't have to share with any neighbors. Vladimir Fedorovich climbed the stairs and pressed the buzzer a few times. Nobody answered, so Vladimir Fedorovich pushed the door, just to see if everything was fine. The door opened and he entered the hallway which led to the living-room. In the penumbra, he could see the mysterious outlines of different objects. A wall-clock was ticking loudly, emphasizing a strange, eerie silence. Vladimir Fedorovich asked in a voice of somebody who was trying in vain to remain calm,

"Is there anybody alive here?"

Nobody alive responded. The clock started ticking more loudly. It now made so much noise that he couldn't hear his own heartbeat. Vladimir Fedorovich felt a tic settle first under one of his eyes and then underneath both of them. Mechanically, he reached for his wooden box when... Even the memory of those events was still terrifying to him, but now, as he was running after Klara along the endless communal hallway towards the cries of rape, he couldn't avoid thinking about them.

Klara also would have liked to avoid dredging up a memory that she had hoped to see buried for good but that now surfaced at the worst moment imaginable, just as she was about to witness a horrible crime. Klara remembered the terrifying game of volley-ball that their team played against a same-year form at their school. Their team was probably the best in the entire city of Kharkov, especially when Klara and Mila Faibusovich came out to the net, shot up and one of them delivered a hit with a piercing scream in a way that made it impossible for anybody to withstand the force of it. The score was 2:2 in that fateful match. The last game of the match, the fifth one, was coming to an end. All they needed was to score a single time more to take the win. The match had been going on for hours. Even the sun looked tired from staying up and following the ball that was passing from one side of the court to the other after being hit by two dozen hands. Finally, the sun yawned and started rolling down the sky to the place where it could count on a well-deserved rest. In its wake, the sun left an uneasy twilight that did not augur any easy solutions... After a serve from the side of the court, Klara and Mila leapt towards the net, soared into the darkened air, and swung their winglike arms. They unleashed a piercing scream that forced the sun to roll down even faster to the protective line of the horizon over the Forest Park. They threw themselves after the ball like two enraged hungry sharks attacking an unsuspecting, harmless little carp...

And that's exactly when a monstrous creature from Klara's childhood tongue-twister ("A big black bug bit a big black dog on his big black nose") emerged from somewhere under the cupboard or the sofa. It moved like a ghost from another world and was bigger than Conan Doyle's hound of the Baskervilles. There was no phosphorous light coming off the creature, which made it even more mysterious.

Vladimir Fedorovich suddenly felt just like that tiny little dog they had seen in the zoo many years ago which only left a wet stain in its wake after a huge dog barked at it. He imagined himself as that wet stain, dropped his wooden box and attempted to stop the tic that had settled underneath both of his eyes. A pitch-black dog whose relatives, as he realized, must have guarded Nazi concentration camps, yawned, as her wolf-like incisors sparkled in the dark, and settled down heavily and menacingly on a door-mat next to the door to the apartment. As Vladimir Fedorovich tried reaching for the wooden box he had dropped, the dog pricked up one of her humongous ears. He picked up the box from the floor and placed it in his pocket with a shaking hand. The dog pricked her other ear that was just as enormous. He stepped towards the door, and the dog sat up. He made another step forward, and the dog rumbled like a bottomless, ravenous stomach. He raised his hand and felt for the switch that would turn on the light when. . .

Mila tried to hit the ball but it was flying too high for her to reach it. The ball was going straight towards Klara's heavy hand. Klara swung her arm so far back that it almost reached her upper spine and hit, or rather, struck, or rather, blasted the black ball that was almost invisible against the darkening sky. This was precisely the way in which Maria had once slapped a sorry admirer who tried to express his liking of her. Klara accompanied her winning serve with a victorious scream of an Amazonian warrior. However. . .

The dog emitted a bark that was so loud that it was heard in the entire apartment, or rather, in the entire building, or rather, in the entire city of Kharkov. It ran towards Vladimir Fedorovich who plopped onto the floor out of sheer terror. The dog placed her paw on his chest, and Vladimir Fedorovich imagined that the dog was getting ready to scalp him and flay him alive...

Instead of plunging down as fast as lightning onto the other team's side of the court, hitting the ground with a thud and bringing Klara's team what turned out to be its long-awaited victory, the ball swayed around like a flower on a stem under a gust of wind and fell down under the net. The untouched ball, in the meanwhile, almost giggled and flew out of bounds. The fans who were still sitting in the bleachers, the other players and the referee gathered around Mila who had been felled by Klara's blow, trying to bring her back to consciousness or at least to figure out if she was still alive. Klara remained standing right where she had landed. Her hand didn't even hurt because of how numb and ice-cold she felt inside. In her thoughts or maybe in a whisper, she kept begging all the saints to keep Mila alive. In the meanwhile. . .

The dog kept her paw on Vladimir Fedorovich's chest. Her endless coil of a tongue was hanging out of her mouth. The animal emitted a snake-like hiss and expectantly observed the door. Finally, the owner came back. He apologized for his tardiness and explained that it had been caused by an electrical failure on the trolley line. Then, he shouted, "Easy, Rex!" and. . .

. . . thank God, Mila got up and said, while rubbing both of the places on her body where she got hurt, "Come on, Klara! We lost such a great game because of you."

"It's a tie!" the terrified referee stuttered. "Gosh, you almost killed me here, girls. One can get a heart attack this way, or something even worse."

"I'd choose a heart attack or something even worse over being hit on one's weakest organ," Mila retorted. Klara was still standing still unable to move. She felt just like that tiny mouse she'd seen in the zoo who had been barked at by a humongous dog.

Looking like somebody who was proud of fulfilling her duty, the dog retreated to her regular place behind the cupboard. Her owner spent quite a while trying to peel Vladimir Fedorovich off the floor.

XX

The scene Klara observed when she arrived in the kitchen made her feel like a character in a cheesy novel. Pipa was reclining against the window-sill and making fruitless efforts to rend the dressing-gown on her heaving chest with a Shakespearian gesture. She was screaming and convulsing. Volkova was approaching her like the Ghost of Hamlet's Father who had materialized in the communal kitchen, with a broken clothes hanger in her trembling hands.

"You did, too!" she kept repeating in a tone of grim condemnation as she pointed the hook of the hanger that looked like a crooked but still accusatory finger at Pipa.

"Rape!!" Pipa objected, wringing her hands and trying to make her gown look like one of a person who was being assaulted.

The very idea of anybody subjecting Pipa to the crime she was announcing at that moment looked quite unrealistic to both Klara and Vladimir Fedorovich. "Scarier than a bombing raid" was a description that applied to her even in her best moments. When Pipa experienced a fit of rage, any assault against her was difficult to imagine, especially if the assailants in question could see what they were doing. Who in their right mind would agree to expose themselves to a bombing raid?

"You did, too!" chanted Volkova who was no more attractive but even tinier than Pipa. She was pointing at her neighbor the clothes hanger that couldn't now even be used to hang a T-shirt.

"Get yourselves under control right now and explain what is going on!" demanded Maria Isaakovna, who had arrived just in time. A woman who feared neither the Dnieper, nor the commission of the Central Committee of the Communist Party, nor the trips to the uranium mines could have hardly been expected to feel intimidated by Pipa and Volkova with her broken clothes hanger. The rest of the neighbors who had gathered round them were visibly shaken.

"Keep your hands to yourselves!" said Vladimir Fedorovich to support his wife and stepped between the angry women and Klara just in case events took an unexpected turn for the worse.

"So?" Maria Isaakovna inquired in a strict and convincing tone of voice. "Have you collected yourselves? Or will you keep hissing like two bacon rashers on a hot pan?"

This unexpected metaphor was appreciated both by the Feldmans who new quite a bit about bacon rashers and by Strelkina who had trouble understanding this image but enjoyed the way the sentence sounded. Klara felt proud of Maria Isaakovna but still couldn't guess what had caused the fight.

In a resigned gesture, Volkova lowered the clothes hanger with its dangling hook, and Pipa stopped rending her clothes. Both of them knew that Maria Isaakovna had been a member of the Comminust Party since 1939 and overall was a person of an important standing not to be messed about with. It is one thing to play an inoffensive prank on somebody but it's a whole different thing to create a horrible scene that includes the infliction of bodily damage and the screaming of unfounded accusations.

"So?" Maria Isaakovna repeated.

Volkova became very respectful and even deferential or, possibly, almost reverential.

"Maria Isaakovna," she said in a tone of somebody who is appealing to a higher authority. "Pipka left her broken clothes hanger under my door. What a jerk, huh? Who knows what she's had hanging on it. Maybe even a roach-infested jacket."

"I'll show you how to call me Pipka," Pipa exploded because her feelings were hurt. "You are a jerk yourself. First you leave it under the door and then you attack me!"

She swallowed some air and added:

"Cow!"

"Silence, all of you!" yelled Maria Isaakovna with the self-assurance of a long-time Party member and the chief engineer of an important project. The women shrank obediently like the German troops under the blows of Marshal Zhukov. "Or better yet, Rokossovsky," Klara thought.

"Now you see, Volkova, how unpleasant it is to find garbage under your door? From now on, quit doing it!"

Volkova opened her mouth and widened her eyes but Maria Isaakovna continued. "And if you, Pipa, keep organizing orgies here, I will have you deported outside the city. Stop crying rape already!"

Pipa sobbed, Volkova snickered, and Maria Isaakovna closed the discussion in what Klara considered to be a very elegant manner.

"This clothes hanger is ours. Give it to me and I will take it out. Volodia, why didn't you take out the garbage as soon as I told you to?"

Vladimir Fedorovich couldn't follow her train of thought but Klara reacted immediately.

"I must have dropped it when I was taking out the garbage."

With her two fingers, she took the half-dead clothes hanger with a hook that was almost falling off, and nodded.

"It surely is ours. Here is a scratch we made on it."

In her mind, she once again quoted Stalin's "They are both worse" as she was looking at her confused neighbors who had no idea why she was smiling.

Klara also thought for some reason that the war was about to end. And then Strelkina would stop occupying the bathroom for so long, Volkova would stop leaving garbage underneath people's doors, and Pipa would not create any more scenes. She felt that she was so sure of this that it made her want to laugh and cry at the same time. And she imagined that everybody wanted to do the same thing. . .

Or maybe she didn't really imagine it but simply something glimmered, flittered in the air, like a pre-war butterfly.

No, it was just something she imagined.

XXI

The spring realized that there was nothing to fear any more, that even though June 22, the anniversary of the war's beginning, was coming soon, it was about to become an inoffensive summer day instead of a scary short night. The spring understood how long people had waited for it to come and, enjoying its own inevitability and trying to make up for such a long absence, it descended, fell, tumbled and cascaded on a Kharkov that sparkled, went crazy and glowed with happiness. Apple-trees, cherry-trees, pear-trees, and apricot-trees at once became covered in white and rose-colored petals.

Kharkov's parks immediately erupted in a laughter of a million trees and shrubs, the grass uncurled its every hidden blade, alleys stopped looking like an old person's wrinkles, park benches again felt like inviting couple to sit on them, cuddle and eat ice-cream. Lemonade stands suddenly sprung up in their old but suddenly renewed places and started offering all of their multi-colored varieties of lemonade.

Kharkov's streets were bursting with happiness. They lost, or rather cast off, happily discarded their erstwhile respectability and started clanking wildly on the curves of the tram routes, prancing around the warm puddles in the asphalt that dried up almost instantly, tap dancing on window-sills and balconies, chirping and singing outside people's windows and begging them not to sleep too late on such an insanely beautiful morning.

Rather, the streets suggested, one should run out into the Sumskaya fast enough to hear the elevator floor thump and its door clank behind you. Then, one should run down the street that had become younger by a whole eternity and follow onto Karazinskaya Street that looks like a first-grader with a huge bouquet of flowers, Mayakovskaya, Chernyshevskaya, the refined Danilevskaya Street, the lofty, albeit tiny, Rymarskaya and down the shabby but still dear to one's heart Klochkovskaya. And, of course, one shouldn't forget to walk along Pushkinskaya, Pushkinskaya, Pushkinskaya, which began to look like Rose-Fingered Maiden must have in the days of her youth. The entire city of Kharkov started looking like a school for noble ladies does after the endlessly boring classes finally end.

Walking, wondering, roaming these streets and listening to the building entrances, passageways, pavements, the trees all of whose branches are performing the First Concerto in which I play the leading part on that white baby-grand piano we had in our pre-war apartment.

"To tell you the truth, Klara, one could hardly get bored by our side," said Mila to distract her friend from her thoughts. This faithful armor-bearer of Klara's found a new topic for discussion and gave a brief dismissive glance to a passerby who tried not to stare at them for too long and who was immediately forgotten by her.

"Why would one get bored by our side?" Klara said in support of her friend's opinion while staring intently at the insanely beautiful Kharkov and paying no attention to the passersby. "We were made for enjoyment, and enjoyment can't be boring."

Mila stopped and asked her suspiciously,

"Whose enjoyment were we made for, in your opinion?"

"Our own," Klara reassured her. "here we are, walking around and enjoying ourselves. Those who want to be bored around us will end up boring us."

They took a turn on Basseinaya and walked by a school. It wasn't their school but, still, it was fine. It bore the number 82, just like Klara's apartment building. Their shadows got tangled in the shadows of happy Kharkov maple-trees and poplars that were glad to take part in the game and mixed Klara's and Mila's shadows with their own.

"Poor Rose-Fingered Maiden," Mila sighed. "First that stupid Rosenblum person makes her suffer with her horrible spelling. . . How is it possible that, at the age of seventeen, one should make two spelling mistakes in a short word like "tunnel"? Not only did she put an "a" instead of a "u" but she also lost an "n."

"I have no idea why one would put just one "n" there. It shortens the tunnel quite a bit."

"True!" Mila laughed. Who needs all those extra adjectives? Just write "tanel" instead of "tunnel", and everybody will realize that the tunnel in question is short and crooked.

Klara stopped to inhale the scent of a white syringa branch. Then, she smelled the lilac one. Then, the white one and the lilac one in turn. Mila did the same. They kept inhaling the aroma and glancing doubtfully at each other and at the shrubs.

"I think they are the same," said Klara tentatively.

"I think the lilac one has a stronger smell," Mila objected in as tentative a manner that must have originated from her natural love of contradiction.

They kept inhaling but the aroma was escaping them.

"We must have gotten used to the scent," Klara concluded regretfully and they continued down the flower-filled street.

"The Rosenblum person, however, is nothing compared to the faculty meetings," Mila continued. "Imagine our poor Maiden having to teach six classes in a row and then suffering through a three-hour-long faculty meeting. Have you heard what happened to her recently? Just before the parade?"

Klara was all attention. Mila paused to make sure her story made a greater impact and waited until her friend said,

"Come on, Milka, out with it."

"Fine, I'll tell you because I know you can keep a secret."

"Cross my heart," Klara confirmed and her pupils widened, turning from grey to dark blue and almost sparkling.

Mila stopped, paused for another decisive moment, gave Klara a terrifying glance, and announced,

"According to reports from my very own news agency, our Maiden entered the tram she takes home from work, adjusted her monocle and commanded the passengers in the same way she does us in class, 'You may be seated now.'"

Klara's pupils widened to unbelievable proportions. For a couple of seconds she stood there trying to digest what she had heard. Having done that, she entered into a clinical fit of laughter. Her blush turned from pale pink to almost purple, tears sprang from her eyes, and her stomach cramped. She bent over, unable to breathe either in or out. The same thing happened to Mila: she contorted and started going in circles around Klara who was frozen in an attack of uncontrollable laughter. At that point, they looked nothing like their school's best athletes and stellar students. Passersby stared at them and, at first, turned away doubtfully, then smiled neutrally and giggled compassionately. Finally, the passersby would start roaring with the infectious laughter, too.

It looked like not only their street but the entire city of Kharkov had gone completely crazy because of how happy everybody was, because of the spring, and because it was finally possible to laugh out loud. They didn't yet know it for sure, but the Victory Day was close, and they could feel it and prepare for it. On that day, an endless and completely different life would begin for them, a life that wouldn't be able to just end. It would be an incomparable, soon-to-begin, endless life.

Klara, Mila and the passersby roared with laughter, and their laughter symbolized this mystical Victory Day that was about to descend not only on Kharkov but onto the entire world, a day they didn't yet know anything about.

The passerby whom Klara had failed to notice a while ago and who had received Mila's withering stare only to be forgotten by her the next moment also didn't yet know anything about that day.

This was how it happened that for the first and the last time ever Klara failed to notice Samuil.

And for the first time ever he didn't fail to notice her.

XXII

Samuil stood there and watch the laughing girl who had turned the corner without noticing him, even though normally people paid attention to him. Not just normally but always. Klara, however, had no time to spare for him because she was busy laughing and smelling the syringa flowers, first the white branch, then the lilac one, then the white one again, and back to the lilac one. She touched the obedient white and pink flowers carefully with the tips of her fingers, trying not to crumple them. Then she would stop and close her eyes for a while, which looked as if she momentarily went to sleep only to awaken in an instant. She was anticipating the soon-to-come day in May that she had been waiting for all this time.

Samuil thought that he hadn't even dreamt of her as he was lugging yet another heavy sack along the endless muddy, snow-covered, dusty road in Arkul. How could he have dreamt of her if he had no idea she was possible? It wasn't about her wavy hair, her smile that was destined only for the trees that had gone crazy over their own and her uniqueness, or her fingers that were touching the lilac bunches that were purring silently under her caress.

It was about all that, of course, but the main thing was that even though Samuil hadn't dreamt of her, he had still seen her somewhere pretty recently. She was simply – or rather, not simply at all – the kind of person that Samuil could neither forget nor remember. . .

He was remembering that he'd seen her somewhere and she looked at him in a way that held his gaze and prevented him from turning away. She looked at him either smiling or studying him, either driving him crazy or consoling him. She was either denying him all hope or extending it.

Right now, however, she was laughing and touching white and lilac flowers on the branches of a shrub, and Samuil didn't feel like comparing her to anyone because there was nobody she could be compared to. In and of itself, any such comparison would necessarily turn out to be a silly and useless thing to do.

She was walking away, towards the Theater Park, and the further she walked away from him, the better he could see her and the more intent he was on figuring out where and when it had been that she stared at him preventing all thought that there might have been hope and inspiring him with courage not to stop hoping.

This is what he was thinking about as he walked along the street and turned the corner.

He kept trying to remember in a tram whose clanging didn't disturb him. His arm was resting on the lowered window pane as the wind attacked him and flitted about the buzzing tram car as if playing hide-and-seek with it. The wind ruffled Samuil's black hair that was slicked back in the same way as that of the famous writer Nikolai Ostrovsky.

XXIII

Klara and Mila always prepared for all the most important tests and exams together and they always did it at Klara's place. It was impossible to concentrate in Mila's apartment even if one shut the door. Her communal apartment neighbors had two nasty dogs who kept barking. One was as huge as a horse, or rather, a stallion, while the other one was a scraggly stray. Unlike Mila, Klara disliked visiting other people's places. Mila, however, always said that a friend's place was even sweeter than home.

Today, they didn't have to go to school. As straight-A students, they were given a day off to prepare for the finals. Tomorrow's final was the worst, in geometry.

Who on earth could possibly enjoy geometry? Parallelograms, ellipses, or even parallelepipeds, God forbid? Who could like these endless triangles that, for some unfathomable reason, kept revolving around their own axis while leaving confusing images in their wake? For how long, might one ask, can one revolve without getting anywhere specific? Just finish revolving once and for all, Klara and Mila thought, and leave people in peace, without the yearly exam whose imminent approach is similar to the advance of enemy armies. The exam had to be passed with an A because neither Klara nor Mila could imagine getting a different grade, even though they suspected that such grades existed.

"A literate human being," Maria Isaakovna would remark in a didactic tone, "should know how to read and write and also possess a spatial imagination."

Of course, it was easy for Maria Isaakovna to say since she did geometry from morning till night with breaks for lunch, sleep, and trips from home to work and back. Mila, however, had little need for this unlovable science.

"A young lady of my massive endowments," objected Mila seriously as she unobtrusively pointed towards some of those endowments, "is not obligated to imagine triangles and tangents."

"In what concerns tangents," Klara added, "I really loathe it when anybody intrudes upon my privacy, even tangentially."

"In what concerns triangles," Mila nodded approvingly, "as for me, Maria Isaakovna, I see myself in silks, not in triangles, including love triangles."

Since the exam was scheduled for the day after, Mila had arrived at Klara's early in the morning. Vladimir Fedorovich was just about to leave for work, so all he had time to do was smile at her and say, "Good morning, Mila. Please come in, Klara has been expecting you."

"Klara, your bosom buddy is here," Maria Isaakovna called out before leaving. She hugged Mila and observed, "You are as punctual and reliable as Sancho Panza."

Mila's eyes adopted the form of circles inscribed into rectangles.

"How can I be a Sancho Panza, Maria Isaakovna? If our most famous movie stars saw my figure, they would have left the scene out of sheer jealousy. Just look at me closely."

"How are your parents doing?" Maria Isaakovna asked with a smile.

"Never better!" Sancho announced. "My Dad can get a new appointment but we don't know anything for sure. So everything is great and getting better."

Maria Isaakovna kissed her and went to the Engineering House to do her eternal geometry while Klara and Mila were left alone to prepare for their test.

"Stand up, Klara," Mila ordered as soon as she entered the room.

Klara did simply because that's what her best and only friend asked her to do. Mila examined her chest attentively, shook her head, and stared at her own chest.

"Not the same," she concluded thoughtfully.

"Mila, have you had a good rest since that horrible volleyball game?" Klara inquired in a voice that was both compassionate and worried. "The one where I missed the ball? Maybe you'll feel better after what they call a peaceful slumber? One's head is not the strongest organ even in the representatives of the weaker sex. . ."

Mila shook her head sadly and explained, "How can we be bosom buddies, Klara, if our bosoms are so different?"

They roared in laughter and proceeded to do their geometry.

XXIV

He didn't visit his parents often because they were very busy trying to make ends meet. At this point, Samuil could hardly be relied upon to help them out. Of course, he was a good student. In a year he was going to be qualified as a mechanic, 2nd class. This was going to take time, however, and in the meanwhile, they had to take care of themselves.

They lived on the outskirts of the city, in a residential area called Balashovka. Semen Mikhailovich worked as a painter at the bicycle factory. Ida worked at the soap factory while Rosa Samoilovna stayed home with her granddaughter. Aunt Sonia, uncle Monia and their son Isia lived nearby. Isia was about to graduate from high school. Uncle Monia worked as a mechanic at the same factory as Semen and also found it hard to make ends meet.

Of course, things weren't all that bad on their quiet street that made one forget this was a big city. It would be great if food was easier to find... For now, they had little hope it would get better any time soon, even though they had one mouth less to feed now that Samuil had moved out. Although I wasn't much of an eater at that time. They say that a person who is six feet tall should weigh at least 150 pounds. My weight – if you can even call it that – was 110 or maybe even 106 pounds.

He wasn't even feeling hungry anymore because when you are always hungry and not a moment goes by when you don't feel hungry, the very notion of hunger loses all meaning. Like if it always was wintertime, that wouldn't be a winter any longer. It would be year-long weather instead. Only when we were given our monthly stipend, my classmates and I could afford to buy stuff and even get some cigarettes.

The longer he had to go hungry – or not even hungry anymore – the less he cared about this stupid hunger and took such high Neapolitan notes when singing and made them last for minutes and not even seconds any more that all the inhabitants of their dorm would go crazy and barge into his dorm room.

Klara, however, – he didn't know yet that she was Klara – did not notice him, even though everybody always did.

Of course, there was also a time when he failed to notice her, even though everybody always did. Only he knew nothing about any of this.

XXV

The quiet was blissful. Nobody was clamoring for access to the bathroom, cries of rape weren't coming from the kitchen, there were no trams under the window. There were a few trolleys but they made no noise. Even if they did, it would hardly be able to reach Klara's fourth-floor window that was located very high. Time was passing in a slow unhurried manner as if aimed at letting one observe the two girls who were different yet quite similar with their wavy black hair and eyes that were protruding just a bit.

"I adore elephants," Mila stretched and looked at the seven snow-white statues of elephants that were ranged by their diminutive sizes in the book-case. "Especially the trunk. I especially adore an elephant's trunk."

"Why the trunk?" Klara enquired in an absent-minded way as she was thinking about the tangents and the circumferences rather than about subjects that were not related to geometry.

Mila crossed her arms on her chest and asked in a strict tone of voice, "And what other part of an elephant's anatomy might be of interest to a respectable young lady? What is it that you, Stolberg, are attempting to suggest to your innocent friend?"

"Dear innocent friend," Klara responded in as strict a tone, "we will discuss your other-worldly innocence at dinner. In the meanwhile, let's go back to studying."

"And what's for dinner?" Mila was fast to wonder.

"Soup with dumplings. . . Milka, stop getting distracted. We still have fifteen more topics to go over. And, by the way, these are not the easiest ones either."

"Did you make the soup yourself?" Mila queried. "Keep in mind, Stolberg, that a dumpling should be more than a piece of dough. Or a glob of dough, like my aunt Basia always says. Have you met my aunt Basia?"

"Any decent person has met your aunt Basia, so how can you even ask? Everybody knows that she is a fount of wisdom, just like our Rose-fingered Maiden."

"Good observation, even though aunt Basia hasn't been a maiden in the literal sense of the term for quite a while. She is also no Rose. That's actually my second-cousin's name. So, as I said, a dumpling should be more than a glob of dough. It should be exciting and tender."

"I can promise it will be tender but there is no guarantee it will excite you. Why are you always so hungry these days?"

"My body is growing," Mila sighed. "It's a good thing it's growing lengthwise and not crosswise. . . I mean, it grows crosswise, too, but only in the right places. As my aunt Basia says, everybody should be so lucky."

"Mila, can you forget about aunt Basia's words of wisdom for a while so that we can go back to studying?"

"As for aunt Basia," Mila continued and then broke off to suggest in an insistent and pleading tone, "why can't we take a break, preferably a long one? All work and no play will make us less exciting than we currently are. So, to continue on the topic of my aunt Basia. She shared a very touching story with me, probably with the goal of edifying me with its help."

"Fine, let's hear it," Klara agreed. "You've got ten minutes to edify us with your story."

"Ten minutes will be more than enough if you don't laugh too hard. The story's title is 'Fornicating Fanny.'"

"What??" Klara managed to mutter in a shaken voice. "Milka, I have a feeling you haven't had enough rest after your sports-related injury. You need to stay in bed and make sure you eat well."

"It's a pity that eating well is quite problematic nowadays," Mila responded and added, "Walls, if you have ears, plug them and let them rest."

After this introduction, she continued her story that promised to be quite piquant, hissing slightly with every "f" sound.

"Fall foliage fluttered faintly. Fornicating Fanny feasted and feted in fennel-flower fields."

Fornicating Fanny came out sinister and salacious at the same time. Klara felt a fit of laughter coming on but managed to resist it for the moment.

"Feeble Father Fallon fondly fondled the fun festive Fanny."

Klara started giggling as Mila continued in a serious, measured tone of voice that lingered on every "f."

"'Fie, Father!' Fornicating Fannie fied flirtatiously."

Klara started laughing uncontrollably, like she always did in such cases.

"Milka, stop it!" she sobbed with laughter but her pitiless Sancho Panza continued,

"Father Fallon forgetfully fingered Fornicating Fanny's fulsome figure."

Here, Mila paused in a way that even the most renowned actress of the day would surely envy and continued,

"Fierce Fanny..."

Klara tried getting from behind the table but laughter made it impossible for her to stand straight.

"... flogged the fiendish..."

Tears of sprang from Klara's eyes.

"... Father Fallon for his fatherly forgetfulness."

Mila bowed down to accept her audience's recognition of her talent while the audience, consisting of a red-faced tearful Klara who was shaking in an uncontrollable fit of laughter, was so incapacitated with mirth as to find it impossible to express its gratitude to the great performer with a round of applause.

"No need to thank me," Mila said with a detached modesty. "Let's just get back to our geometry."

"Let me be," Klara managed to squeeze out as she crawled over to the sofa and wiped her tears on a cushion.

In the evening, after Maria Isaakovna and Vladimir Fedorovich had come home from work, they had dinner together, praising Klara's dumpling soup. As usual, Vladimir Fedorovich said, 'Thank you so very much." Then, Klara went to see Mila home and asked her,

"Milka, do you agree that no happiness exists, just force of will and peace?"

Mila shrugged her shoulders and responded with an air of condescension,

"Pushkin was a great poet, of course, but why do you have to offend me with this quote?"

Klara raised her brows in astonishment,

"Come on, how did I offend you?"

"You and I had a whole day of happiness, and an evening, too. And then you go and doubt if happiness exists."

XXVI

They all, Klara, Samuil, Mila, Maria Isaakovna, Vladimir Fedorovich, all of their relatives and neighbors and every single person around them, were waiting impatiently for the most important Day of all. They were sure that when that Day came, everything would become as wonderful as it had never been before. They all had dreams of their own but their main hope was the same: that the war would end.

The main thing was that the war would end.

The war would end.

They repeated this wish and this exhortation, this first and foremost request so often that it had become almost a prayer and they were prepared to give all they still had and all they still didn't have to make sure that this all-important wish finally came true.

This was the first and the last holiday that they awaited not because they knew how wonderful it was but, rather, because they'd never had a holiday like this one. It was coming closer, approaching, drawing near, inching towards them like a bird of passage that was on its way back home. And they were afraid of scaring it off by their loud – almost out loud – screaming desire, their barely audible raging prayer. Just let it come and stay, and after that let come what may. . .

Such a Holiday could only take place in spring. If spring didn't exist and if the month of May wasn't part of it, this Holiday would not have come about. If it weren't for the spring that had unleashed itself over Kharkov, over their entire country, over the whole wide world, this Holiday wouldn't have found a place for itself. It was too huge to fit itself into any other month, and what would become of all those other months without the month of May?

All through this most important day, her heart beat so fast that she felt she was back in her childhood and Mom had left for work or maybe went on a business trip and she wanted to go outside and was knocking, banging, pummeling on a locked door that wouldn't open, but she still believed that a miracle would happen and the door would somehow open...

All through this most important day, he felt he was back behind his lathe, working on a part which just wouldn't come out right. And as hard as you try, it still remains an ingot, a senseless bar of metal under a cloud of sparkles that you can't manage to turn into the shape it has to take, but he still believed that a miracle would happen and the ingot would suddenly acquire the needed shape.

And then the miracle they had all awaited, dreamed about, prayed for finally happened. The month of May arrived, and the bird of passage that had found its way home returned out of nowhere. It flew over Dzerzhinsky Square, waving its wings at everybody who survived and was now crying beneath it in a way that made little sense: how can you cry on a day like this? The bird had thought that by arriving it would make them happy, but, for some reason, all of the millions of survivors raised their heads and wept as if they couldn't make themselves believe that their bird of passage had finally come back to them. Or maybe they wept because they could finally believe it.

And then, suddenly, a roar of thunder came from behind the Gosprom, or the marketplace, or maybe the Shatilovka suburb. It was the kind of thunder that no past month of May had seen or could have possibly seen. A gust of an unbelievable hurricane seemed to have torn the pink, white and lilac flowers off the tree-branches that were as overcome with happiness and that were weeping together with everybody else and threw the flowers into the dark purple sky that they lit up like no stars ever could. These flowers soared towards the sky like sparkles coming out of a lathe, and then an unseen, unimaginable piano that was accompanied with an unheard of orchestra thundered with the First Concerto. The stars lingered in the sky, looked down at the people who were weeping and laughing at the same time, and fell into the millions of stretched out hands as millions of May bouquets.

XXVII

This holiday continued even on the next day. A lazy, burnished sun that looked like an imposing vessel rose from behind the Forest Park. It floated towards Klara's balcony and paused over it reluctant to leave without catching a glimpse of apartment seven and finding out how much things had changed there.

Everything had, indeed, changed, even though one didn't care to think how long the change would last. Be that as it may, Strelkina abstained from occupying the bathroom for her customary forty minutes, Volkova didn't leave any rubbish underneath anybody's door, and Pipa said nothing when Klara ran into the kitchen and kissed her on the cheek. She kissed not only Pipa but also the Feldmans, and before that, of course, Maria Isaakovna and Vladimir Fedorovich. This morning she would have even kissed Marik but, thankfully, he wasn't around on that morning.

Finally, the sun managed to see her when Klara emerged onto the balcony. In front of her and beneath her, the naively majestic, old-fashioned Sumskaya Street stretched itself in a way that was as imposing as the floating sun. The street was renewed by the morning water-sprinklers and it lied there remembering – how it could ever forget? – the carriages that passed down it at the precise moment when Klara left her house in Rechitsa – here she is, can't you see her? She is turning the door-knob of her house's gate, comes outside into a street in Rechitsa that smells of apples and geese. Here she is, at this very moment, stumbling over a piece of gravel. I wonder, what kind of footwear is she wearing? She laughs because nothing seems like that big of a deal when one is just sixteen years of age, flips her wavy black hair that doesn't need to be covered with a kerchief when the weather is this warm.

Here she is, so beautiful that the entire town of Rechitsa has started going crazy over her, fun-loving, fast, noticing everything around her and having her own opinion about everything she sees. Her opinions are always the only correct ones, even though on the next day they can transform into their opposite, but still the only correct ones for the simple reason that they are her own. She, Klara, is completely unique. Stars are many and they all look alike (and it isn't much of a look, too, to be completely honest.) Who cares that there are so many of them in the sky when here there is only one me?

Even her name was unlike anybody else. She wasn't a Rose who'd lose all her petals at the smallest gust of wind. She wasn't a Rachael, and what kind of a weird name was that, anyway? Nor was she a Sarah which was an OK name but still, everybody who wasn't a Rose, a Rachael, or a Rivka – that's what one really needed, another Rivka! – turned out to be named Sarah.

There is one and only Klara, though, and it's obvious that it's me. Haya sounded fine, even kind of majestic. Mary, too. If one couldn't be called Klara, the only way to go was to be named Mary.

Here she is, Klara, walking down a street in Rechitsa, lost in thought, arguing with herself. Here she is, this very second, can't you see her? No, she isn't underneath Klara's balcony, on the Sumskaya Street that has been freshened up by morning sprinklers. Here she is, walking past Isaak Krupetsky, the most interesting guy in the entire town of Rechitsa, and Isaak looks at her in a way that leaves no room for doubt. She looks back at him without averting her gaze (for Klara to avert her gaze?) and smiles at him with her condescending royal smile that makes him feel like a gasping gudgeon on the bank of the Dnieper River. Here she comes, right here. Now she has seen – and what an eye-sight she's got! – Klara on her balcony of the ancient building number eighty-two, on the fourth floor, and is calling out to her,

"Good morning, my lovely daughter!"

"Whose daughter?" Klara wondered and flicked the black waves of her hair that soared up and rushed down like yesterday's interminable fireworks.

Why daughter?

The Sumskaya Street also shook itself up to help her out, while the sun did its part by placing itself as an orange wedge right in front of her. Klara saw Zinovi Stolberg standing on the pavement underneath the balcony. He was holding three red carnations in one hand and a small package wrapped in a newspaper in the other.

"Daddy!" Klara exclaimed and rushed from her balcony to the sparkling pavement. The elevator's floor bumped, the door clanged behind her back, and Klara was inhaling the scent of the red carnations that smelled of nothing but still managed to smell beautifully. She was trying to understand what was had happened to Zinovi's right hand that was missing three of its fingers.

"Don't worry," he said to make her feel better and unwrapped the newspaper. A dagger in a grey steel sheath emerged from the package. It had a pompom that looked almost childish and a black plastic handle that was missing a piece."A bullet fragment hit it at the very moment when I was going to make use of it for the first time."

They sat on a bench under an ancient but still not very old oak that stood next to the monument to the poet Shevchenko. Klara removed the dagger from its sheath. It was thick and had a curved blade with a meticulous German stamp that said "Messerschmitt."

"Dad, how was it over there? Was it scary?" Klara asked.

"What's scary is how pleasant it is to sit on a bench in Shevchenko Gardens with one's grown daughter," Zinovi smiled and kissed Klara's black mane of hair. "Who else has such a beautiful grown-up daughter? I wouldn't mind having such a granddaughter, too."

"I will have a son," Klara said. "Which means you will have a grandson."

They kept silent for a while. Klara wanted to ask something but Zinovi spoke first.

"Klara, are you going to college this year or the next?"

Klara nodded, "The next."

"Have you decided where you will apply?"

"The university, I think. The Department of Philology, or maybe the Foreign Languages."

Zinovi returned the dagger into its sheath and re-wrapped it in the newspaper.

"How about the entrance examinations?"

"I will be awarded a gold medal for my academic excellence, so entrance exams will not be required. There are more than enough finals for me to pass before I can graduate high school. There are thirteen of them altogether."

A seemingly accidental cloud sprinkled with a bit of rain and immediately hurried away in a playful manner towards either the Southern railway station or the Cold Mountain.

"Dad, was it scary over there?" Klara asked again gazing into Zinovi's eyes.

Zinovi smoked, holding the cigarette in his intact hand, and silently stared at the stone statues that circled the monument to Shevchenko, at the freshly washed Sumskaya Street, and at the Engineering House that towered over the chestnut lane.

"You know, sweetheart," he said very quietly, "there is this kind of feeling that is worse than fear. I don't know what to call it but it's scarier than fear. It was scary when our entire platoon was marching together and each of us prayed that we wouldn't be bombed by a German plane. The entire formation marched onto a bridge across a river. I was the last in line, so I didn't get a chance to reach the bridge. Then, a German plane came and dropped a bomb onto the bridge. And they all disappeared. If I had gotten onto the bridge, I would have died, too. So there I was, standing on the river-bank, looking at the water, with my platoon all gone. I was standing there unable to make any sense of what had happened. A moment ago, they were all there, all nineteen soldiers, right there, in that very place, and all of a sudden they were all gone."

Klara was clutching and unclutching the newspaper-wrapped package without realizing it.

"I'd rather be afraid than experience something like that," Zinovi said.

They were silent for a long while, or for what seemed like a long while to them. . . Then, Klara said,

"The present keeps becoming the past. . . You can barely turn around, and it has all turned into the past. . ."

Zinovi laughed in a comforting way and hugged her.

"That depends on where you are looking from, sweetheart. If you look from where you are right now, then you are right, the past is what used to be a future at some point. However, if you look from the bygone time, then there is no past. There is just the present that is preparing to become a future."

Klara smiled and caressed his hand that was missing three of its fingers, while Zinovi added,

"When things get really bad. . . Does that ever happen to you?"

Klara shook her head.

"Good for you. In case it does happen, though, never look backwards. It's like looking downwards from a mountaintop. . ."

He paused for thought and added,

"The best thing you can do - and this is the most reliable piece of advice I can give you - is to find something that makes you happy, even if it's a tiny little thing, and try making it grow, expand and conceal all of your troubles behind it."

"Do you manage to do that?" Klara asked.

Zinovi burst out laughing again,

"Why wouldn't I? How can you and I possibly fail at anything we propose to do? That's the only thing I can't imagine happening!"

A grave colleague of the cloud that had floated away towards the Cold Mountain or the Southern railway station appeared from behind the Gosprom sky-scraper. Its shape and color reminded one of a bruise. Zinovi kissed Klara on the blush that appeared above her dimples.

The elevator thumped and clanged once again, and Vladimir Fedorovich asked with a smile,

"So whom did you disarm today?"

"I went out with Dad," Klara answered, as she removed the somewhat crooked blade from the sheath with a pompom.

Maria Isaakovna was appalled.

"This Stolberg person always comes up with something silly. Who gives a cleaver to a kid?"

"It is a trophy dagger, Mom," explained Klara in a tone that admitted no contradiction. "See how an explosion took out a chunk of it?"

Maria didn't see it and had no desire to see anything of the kind. There were so many things she needed to do that there was no time or energy left to think about some rusty cleaver with its Stolberg. She couldn't even think of Stolberg as a stage in her life because, in truth, her life had begun after their separation.

So much was yet ahead of her, it seemed, that anything could happen to her life except that it could never end.

XXVIII

He was so hungry that it even made him laugh, although there was hardly any energy left for laughing. Samuil used these last remnants of energy to drag himself towards the day when he would graduate from his vocational school and finally apply to med school. He had already learned how to repair pretty much any leaky faucet, replace worn seals, shape any detail on his lathe, except the most elaborate ones, of course. Any factory or housing department would hire him in a flash. But he had spent half of his life wanting to become a doctor. He didn't just dream of it. He wanted it, which is why it was impossible to stop him.

Of course, he still had to pass the entrance examinations, may they rot in hell together with those who administer them. The Ukrainian language exam he could pass easily. Physics was doable. He knew that if an A was unattainable, he could get at least a B or maybe a B-. Chemistry, however, was the main, or rather, the only horror. Samuil had nothing against chemistry itself. He was sure that there must have been people who found it useful for whatever purposes of their own. But what use could it have for a practicing physician? To develop drugs? For one, medication was developed by pharmaceutical concerns, not by doctors like himself. At the same time, drugs never cured anything. In the best-case scenario, they just drove the disease deeper towards its source.

A doctor shouldn't stuff a patient full of pills. His job is to teach the patient how to become healthy and remain healthy. He must force him – yes, force him, if necessary – to believe that he can be cured and explain what he needs to do to avoid falling sick again. He must teach the patient not to overeat, not to drink, sleep, lie and sit too much. The most important thing is to be constantly on the move. And it's just as crucial to be in a good mood. Most diseases come when one gets despondent. The moment you start feeling hopeless you can expect to get sick. A disease will find a weak spot in your body if you help it do that. If you don't want to help out the disease, try helping out your doctor instead. Smile or, better yet, laugh. Roar out with laughter. Enjoy life. Don't just sit there or lie there like a log. What can be better than life? So celebrate it, no matter what it brings.

Samuil wanted to study. He wanted real doctors to teach him how to cure people. He wanted to be told of great healers, of miraculous cures. Cures that were done with the help of a word, not a drug, new methods of healing. All those silly chemical reactions of replacement, reduction, evaporation, exclusion, inclusion, though, might be useful to somebody else but not to him who had spent half of his life hoping to cure people. They were similarly useless to his patients who were kept waiting for their doctor to finally be allowed to cure them and teach them how to lead healthy loves.

Samuil was a good student. He had excelled at his secondary school in Voroshilovgrad and even now, had it not been for constant hunger pangs, could have overcome both physics and even this useless chemistry. The hunger was always there, however, which left him with little energy to laugh and even sing...

And most importantly, Klara wasn't to be found on Basseinaya Street any longer...

XXIX

Maria had taken Klara away to the Riga Beach. It was her plan to fortify the kid's health before the decisive graduating year of high school. In order to get a gold medal – which was the only possibility Maria allowed for – Klara had to pass all thirteen of the final exams with the grade of "A". Truth be told, Klara was always a straight A student, just like her mother had been, in Kharkov, at the Urals, and back in Khrakov again. Still, thirteen finals were hardly a walk in Kharkov's Forest Park.

Subjects like Constitution of the USSR or Russian, for example, were easy. Chemistry or trigonometry, however, were hard even for Klara, which is why Maria thought it was necessary to fortify the kid's health. Eating well also mattered a lot. Of course, nobody had ever taken care to fortify Maria when she was a kid but that was a long time ago and there wasn't anything good about that anyways.

They had a dream, or, rather, a goal, which meant that the result was predetermined: their family was going to have three medals instead of just two like they had now. Maria Isaakovna and Vladimir Fedorovich had been awarded medals "For Heroic Achievement" that were decorated with a portrait of Stalin and the words "We Will Prevail." The portrait looked like the white bust in their bookcase. Whenever Klara looked at these medals, she remembered the same documentary that neither she nor Maria Isaakovna nor Vladimir Fedorovich nor their neighbors, the Feldmans and Pipa included, could ever forget. The documentary showed the Red Square parade in November 1941 where Stalin said to the soldiers,

"Let the banners of the invincible leaders Suvorov and Kutuzov bless you."

Klara would stare at these medals and imagine a bomb hitting the bridge that Zinovi's friends hadn't managed to cross, leaving him alone with nobody else to save Klara who had been lost on her way home from school.

Now Klara was going to have a medal of her own, the third medal their family would get. The medal would be big, made of gold, not copper, with an open book etched on its surface. All that was left for her to do was finish her last year of high school and pass the thirteen finals with a grade of "A". You think that's easier than design the biggest electric power plant in the world? Or send several thousand military trains to the battlefield?

Still, the most important thing was that Samuil wasn't to be found on Rymarskaya Street any longer. He wasn't on the Riga Beach either: they had left the place a long time ago. Of course, she didn't know about it at this point. And before, she wouldn't have paid any attention to him.

XXX

Klara and Mila turned the corner of Chernyshevskaya Street for the last time: Mila's father had been posted to the far-away city of Vladivostok.

The heat had emerged every nook and cranny, and it was stuffy and unwelcoming. Mila bore the armor with dignity, as usual. She was telling a thousand and one stories about the notorious Rosenblum person, about some completely unknown characters, about the Rose-fingered Maiden, and about some older but still quite spry guy named either Liova or Lionia who had looked at Mila as a woman.

"Hell froze over, cows flew by and pigs grew wings," Mila said. "What can one do if a man of an advanced age has a sophisticated taste and has decided to perform his own swan's song?"

"What and who are you talking about?" asked Klara with interest but already imagining how Chernyshevskaya Street would look without Mila there. She would have to learn to bear her own armor now.

"My parents and I went to visit our friends," Mila continued evincing a similar degree of interest but trying to imagine Chernyshevskaya Street without herself and herself without her best friend. "And there was this guy called either Liova or Lionia who dared to regale me – imagine that! – with a knowing glance. Of course, I don't begrudge him this rare joyous moment. Let him experience a naked instance of untold bliss."

Klara really wanted to stop imagining now but Chernyshevskaya Street kept getting emptier while the embankment in the city of Vladivostok wasn't getting any more populated either. So why did it have to happen at all? Who had decided that it was time and that anybody would be better off this way?

"So this Liova or Lionia guy," Mila kept narrating, "devoured me with a glance that has rusted as a result of its long-time lack of appeal..."

Klara wanted to burst out crying but Chernyshevskaya Street was so senselessly empty that one didn't even have any energy left for crying. Mila got herself together and continued, "I let him know that while his impressions were correct, his expectations were tragically mistaken."

"Exactly," Klara nodded with difficulty. "These guys let their eyes roam all over the place. One can hardly find a place to hide from all their lard."

Mila made such an effort not to let Klara see how much she hated the stupid empty Chernyshevskaya Street that her bones almost cracked. She continued her story, "And as to my Mom, well, you know that Mom gives her all to the defense of morality..."

"As if you'd perform some action that would be offensive to her morality, if she didn't give it her all," said Klara as she almost gave in to the desire to burst out crying.

"Precisely. My mother flared up and said, or rather, puffed, at my aunt Basia – you know my aunt Basia, don't you?"

"How could I possibly fail to know your aunt Basia?" Klara responded as if speaking from a different street.

Chernyshevskaya creaked and prickled her feet. The part of the road where the shadows of the trees did not reach had turned into a viscous shoe polish. And at that very same moment, Klara – here she is, right now – was removing from the stove a frying-pan with delicious latkes, Vladimir Fedorovich's favorite dish that he called potato pancakes. Today, they are expecting visitors. The Krupetskys had promised to come by. Let Isaak try her latkes with their crispy crust, let him try them and look at Klara in a different way than he does when they run into each other in the street. Of course, she likes it when he looks at her this way, she really does, but let him look at her in a different way, too. And then we'll see what happens. Here she is, placing the frying-pan on the table, and her mother exclaims, "Oy veiz mir, bubbala! Don't be putting it on the table like that. Just place it on a mat."

And Dad is saying, "Az och und vey, if the child has made latkes once in a blue moon, let her put them wherever she wants. Leave the child be, can't you?"

Mila and Klara go their separate ways in the meanwhile and Mila says by way of a good-bye,

"And my Mom – get that! – tells aunt Basia... you know my aunt Basia, right?"

"Milka, I know your aunt Basia," says Klara almost on the verge of tears. "Why are you persecuting me with your aunt Basia, az och und vey, really!"

Mila was shaken by everything that had happened and the fact that Klara had suddenly lost her eighteenth-century manners shook her even more. So she finished her story, which had promised to be as fascinating as usual, in a plaintive and helpless way,

"Mom said, 'Basia, only imagine, he looked at her as a woman!'

And aunt Basia responded, just like King Solomon,

'Come on, Fira, do you want your daughter to be looked at as a man? Can your daughter, peace be onto her, really be interpreted that way?'"

Klara and Mila stopped in the middle of Chernyshevskaya Street which now looked either hale or hearty. And the street that used to be endless suddenly ended. It remained empty behind their backs, as if nothing had ever been there, except what they imagined or dreamt of. Klara, in the meanwhile, had found a mat for her frying-pan, removed her new purple kerchief that had been tied properly on the nape of her neck and looked proudly at her parents. She had no idea that Chernyshevskaya Street had become as senseless as a consumed potato pancake. And Klara just didn't care about anything anymore. She burst out crying like the silliest fool ever. Mila dropped her armor onto the slurping pavement and burst out crying as loudly, while she tried to console her friend, "Klarka, don't be an idiot, Vladivostok is much closer than the North Pole..."

Klara had never wept before, even in the Urals. Mila hadn't wept either, even when Klara had hit her head instead of hitting the ball. This is why now their weeping was especially hard, just like Zinovi had warned Klara.

"We'll meet some day," offered Mila just to say something.

Klara stopped hugging her for a moment and squeezed out an inevitable,

"Idiot!"

Mila looked petrified. She finally understood what was going on and responded with just as inevitable,

"Idiot yourself!"

And they burst out weeping so loud that the entire Chernyshevskaya Street that had just eneded for them once and for all could hear them.

Passers-by were probably thinking, "Are these the same girls that back in spring were smelling syringe flowers and laughing like crazy?"

And then they answered their own question with, "No, these must be different girls."

XXXI

A B in physics didn't look bad at all. To be completely honest, it looked good, just like it supposed to. Chemistry that had been invented by learned scholars loomed ahead of him, and that's where he could only hope for a B. . . Well, let come what may, or whatever they say in such cases. If others managed to do it, so could he. But for the time being he could relax and forget about the stupid, useless exams, especially since there were no volunteers in sight willing to listen to his story of how he'd passed the physics exam without even using a cheat sheet.

Samuil inhaled the hot air one could almost cut with a knife and sauntered in a leisurely manner away from the Medical School that was as yet inaccessible to him down the Trinkler Street, Dzerzhinsky Square and Sumskaya Street where they had started building something like a weird cabin or maybe a monument. He walked down Chernyshevskaya Street that was as empty as a sheet of a brand-new notebook. Then, because he had nothing else to do with his time, he strolled towards the corner where, at the turn of the tram route number five, there was the beautiful, pre-revolutionary building of the Law School.

He had run out of cigarettes, and a single almost smoked-down cigarette butt was all he had left. His empty pockets contained no money for a fresh pack but Samuil cared little about that. The only thing that mattered was that he never had to cram for and pass the stupid physics exam ever again, which meant that he could gladly erase from his memory not only everything that had to do with it but even the very fact of its existence.

For some reason, he kept walking towards the Law School building, staring with a smile at the puffing and huffing passers-by, and sang soundlessly a Neapolitan song he'd learned a short while ago. Passers-by didn't seem to appreciate the sight of this guy who paid no attention to the intense heat and just strolled with his hands in his pockets, with his shirt unbuttoned, smiling incomprehensibly to himself.

I don't know, it looked like any regular street, but a girl that was impossible to imagine walked down it onto Chernyshevskaya Street. She was impossible to imagine because I'd never imagined a girl like her, which means that now I never will imagine her again. . .

XXXII

The university disappointed her, even though she only saw a small part of it. In the morning, Klara had invested forty precious minutes into her appearance. In order to do that, she managed to get to the bathroom before Strelkina occupied it. Strelkina had to spend fifteen minutes pacing desperately in front of the bathroom but never dared to express her resentment towards Klara. When she emerged from the bathroom, Klara pointed to a cobweb above Strelkin's door that was located right in front of the bathroom. Then, she pointed towards herself and unapologetically announced,

"Cleanliness is proletariat's best weapon. Cleanliness and not a paving stone, comrades!" After that, she went back to her room to put on a chic dress that had been made for her to wear to the university by Fira Markovna Feldman. "Chic" was not, of course, a word Klara used. It was what her mother called the dress. However, if one were to be honest, the dress's creamy color, its shoulder line and its waist were worthy of their wearer, to use Klara's terminology.

"The wearer and what is being worn," declared Klara before the fitting, "should be in harmony with each other, like a couple of newlyweds who are madly in love. They should never remind one of a couple of old fogeys who are sick and tired of each other."

"Are you satisfied?" asked Maria with a well-concealed glee that only Klara could notice.

"Mommy, you and I are both not just satisfied but truly happy," Klara responded and showered Fira Markovna, her tailor magician, with kisses.

Vladimir Fedorovich kept silent and just smiled because he knew that nobody else had the kind of daughter that he did. There was nobody to give a lollipop to any longer but the rest remained unchanged. He looked at Klara, smiling and thinking that, while he could, he will not let things change.

There were now three medals in their family. The one Maria Isaakovna and Vladimir Fedorovich cherished the most – big, made of pure gold, and depicting a book open on Klara's favorite passage from *War and Peace* – was kept in a box in one of the drawers in the wardrobe.

Klara kissed everybody who was seeing her off, rushed as fast as a bullet into the elevator on her fourth floor, emerged from it on the first floor to the accompaniment of the customary clang and thump, and headed directly to the University Hill. She took a less comfortable route, along Rymarskaya Street, which, however, was as empty as Chernyshevskaya. As usual, there were crowds of people that ambled back and forth puffing and huffing like thousands of badly polished tea-kettles.

The university, however, disappointed her, even though she only saw a small part of it. The male representatives of the student body at the Department of Philology (the Department of Foreign Languages only had female students) were only remarkable for their klutziness and schmaltziness. Klara imagined the range of emotions that any of the thousand writers she had read would experience at the sight of these future scholars of their literary production. That made her dislike the very idea of becoming one of them.

The Department of Foreign Languages also failed to inspire her. The unhealthy preponderance of an annoyingly weaker sex that was sweating in the expectation of the inevitable doom offered a future of unavoidable repetition of seemingly irregular verbs whose conjugations she had learned a long time ago. It also augured endless discussions of strategies that would help one get married which both linguistically and philosophically evoked an image of a calm and proud male invested with the power of bestowing the gift of marriage on a female who had to work hard not to let this kind of happiness slip away.

The sun had also begun to sweat as a result of its own heat, and the sky covered itself with a dry fog. Klara sighed contentedly, feeling sorry for the university that now had no chance of getting her to become a part of it. She mused that everything that happened was for the better and turned back, walking through the same empty, people-filled Rymarskaya Street and towards Tevelev Square that Vladimir Fedorovich always referred to as St. Nicholas Square. Then she headed towards Pushkinskaya Street and, for some reason, wandered in the direction of the Law School that was located in a luxurious building constructed by Becketov during the reign of one of the two most recent Tsars who bore the name of Alexander.

XXXIII

In the meanwhile, Samuil entered the little square in front of the Law School because there was little else to do in such hot weather.

Suddenly – all of a sudden and completely out of the blue – he saw the reason why Chernyshevskaya and all other streets had seemed so empty. Now, however, it stopped mattering and he couldn't care less about them any longer for the simple reason that the girl who had turned the corner on Chernyshevskaya Street and paid no attention to Samuil (why should she have, anyways?) was now standing just a few feet away and didn't look like she was planning to go anywhere.

To the contrary, she was explaining some math to a group of lieutenants and captains who were much older and, at a minimum, could pass for her elder brothers. The twenty or so officers were hot but not so much because of the heat and their heavy uniforms but, rather, because of the math. They were failing to grasp it for two reasons. First, math was notoriously hard to understand, especially after a long break like the one they'd had. Second, and most importantly, the girl had the kind of eyes, smile and dimples that one could barely concentrate on the math. . .

The prospective students at the Law School turned out to be quite different. There were no girls of marriageable age and no schmaltzy Mamma's boys either. Instead, lieutenants who had just come home from the battlefield were applying to the Law School because they wanted to become investigators and prosecutors. Their knowledge was limited, which was very understandable, but in the five years it would take them to get their diplomas, they would catch up and learn all they needed. At least, they had everything else: after what they'd been through, there were no serious obstacles left ahead of them.

Klara's papers were in her handbag and it took her just a couple of minutes to get admitted to the Law School. She already knew that she was going to become an attorney as famous as the fabled lawyer Plevako. Then, she returned to the square to help out the officers who were the most terrified of the math and the composition, which were pretty much all there was.

Samuil was afraid we would remain riveted to the ground as if weighed down by the heaviest sack of flour from Arkul. He inhaled, exhaled, then inhaled once again, and finally decided to come closer.

This was when Klara realized why Rymarskaya Street had seemed so empty. Now it stopped having the slightest importance, though, since a skinny guy with his black hair slicked back in the manner of the famous writer Nikolai Ostrovsky and with a burning smile was sauntering right towards them, as if the group of friends in whose company he had been laughing so hard a year and a half ago had suddenly stopped being enough for him. This time, Klara got a much better look at him and realized that he was capable of not just overcoming but actually pushing through any obstacle. Not because the obstacle would turn out to be insignificant, but rather because he wouldn't even notice it.

The girl gave him a look that was sobering and unapproachable. Samuil felt that he didn't know what to do. It would have been intolerable for him not to look at her because he had already spent too much time not looking, but it was equally unacceptable to continue staring. It would be fine if she were simply beautiful. The girl he was in love with in Arkul and his episodic Kharkov paramours were easy on the eyes, too. Not to this extent, of course, but more or less so. This girl, however, had the kind of stare that made one feel like a thread had bound him and tugged him in her direction. The thread felt like it could break all of a sudden, which would make the streets become empty again, this time forever. This wasn't all, though. The most important thing was that he suddenly remembered where he had seen her, which made him muse sadly,

"Doctor, cure thyself because it seems like you are going crazy here." His legs refused to carry him any further at this point, and he wasn't even sure any more if he had legs. How could anybody refer to these cotton wool crutches as legs?

As he approached the group in a few long, firm strides, the guy smiled like the actor Utesov in a famous movie and said, paying no attention to the officers, albeit in a manner that wasn't rude at all, "I've been looking for you."

Samuil excused himself and muttered something polite to those present. In the meanwhile, he was looking at Klara and hoping that the thread that stretched between them wouldn't break, allowing him to come up with something funny and light that would be of interest to her.

"I knew that some dark forces were following me. I thought it was the figment of my female imagination but it seems like I was right. How come I failed to notice anybody observing me? Of course, you are so skinny you could hide behind a flag-pole."

"Your name isn't Maria, is it, Ma'am?" Samuil asked in a clumsy way.

"Maria is my mother's name. Would you like to meet her? I don't promise that talking to her will be easy but I can at least introduce you. My name is Klarissa. Klara, for short. What's yours? Just don't call me 'Ma'am' because that makes me feel like your former school-teacher."

"Samuil," he said and stretched his hand towards Klara.

"It is up to a lady to initiate a handshake and only if she chooses to," Klara responded. "Have you noticed which one of us is a lady?"

Samuil tried to say something and Klara nodded her approval,

"The suspect should always be given the benefit of the doubt. Here, in Pushkin Entry, is where we lived before the war. Mom, Vladimir Fedorovich, and I. We were evacuated to the Urals. They worked all day long while I went to school, also all day long. What did you do during the war? Study?"

"No, you see, I didn't get a chance to study because I had to work to feed the family. I had finished the seventh grade back in Voroshilovgrad. But in Arkul I had no time to study because I had to carry flour sacks from the mill to the bakery. Twenty kilometers there and back."

"So how old were you then?"

"I was fifteen when I started and seventeen by the end of it. There is nothing much to be proud of here. This is what the war was like. You know that yourself."

"I do. . . And now what do you do?"

"I'm trying to get into Med School. I just finished the vocational school and can do any kind of manual labor. I want to be a doctor, though. If only stupid chemistry didn't get in the way. . . You see, I can't just cram if I don't understand the purpose of cramming."

"Well, how about C_2H_5OH? Doesn't a doctor need to know what it means?"

"Az och und vei," as my father would say. "Why should a doctor know this kind of silly stuff? As if it really mattered. If my hospital needs a hundred liters of pure alcohol, I will simply order one hundred liters of pure alcohol. They should just tell me where I can order it and stick the information about how it was invented up their. . . Excuse the language."

"Don't worry, I know where you'd like them to stick it. For many people, that's a s good destination as any. As my best friend's aunt used to say, a great tuches is a great naches. If you'd like, I can help you."

"Are you good with chemistry, too?"

"I'm good with everything. I was awarded a gold medal and yesterday I was accepted to Law School. I decided to become a lawyer."

"And I'll be a doctor, and those who don't like it can go hang themselves."

"Nobody will need to hang themselves. Anyways, Senia, don't think of anything other than chemistry right now."

"Chemistry is the last thing on my mind."

"Playfulness and flirtatiousness are hardly appropriate when you are about to compete with ten other people for a place in Medical School."

"Here is where I remember seeing you. You were smelling flowers on the syring-bush and the apple-tree. You were laughing like crazy, too."

"Mila must have told me one of her stories. She used to be a great story-teller. . ."

"Has she died?"

"Bah, of course not! They moved to Vladivostok. . . And this is where I saw you for the first time. You were also telling something funny to your friends, just like Milka used to do."

"This must have been when we went out to have some beer."

"I have nothing against alcohol if one knows one's limit. The question remains if it makes sense to try to reach that limit."

"Klara, listen, why is the ferris wheel called ferris? Was it invented by somebody called Ferris? Or is it because it often appears at fairs?"

"That's what I've been missing! First, an unintelligent question and then . . . like it's been my childhood dream to be licked by an ash-tray."

"I'm sorry, I won't do it anymore. It's just a force of habit. . . Sorry, I didn't mean that the way it came out! . . What I wanted to say was that. . ."

"Samuil, I don't want to feel like you are sticking a cigarette butt in my mouth. So please just take measures against that happening in the future. That is, if you are counting on there being a future."

"Hello, darling Klara," Maria Isaakovna said, ignoring Samuil. She was much shorter than he was, which did not prevent her from towering over him like the fire lookout tower over a bar on Sverdlov Street.

XXXIV

"Mother," Klara said in a compassionate but strict tone of voice, "please meet Samuil."

"It's great to meet you," lied Samuil and offered her a smile so wide as if he was at the chemistry exam with no knowledge of how to answer a single question.

Maria Isaakovna went over Samuil's face in the same way as a recent hail storm went over the city of Kharkov. Her chiffon scarf moved and whispered something very quietly.

"It's great to meet you, too." She declared and moved her gaze over to Klara. "Sweetheart, Marik just called. He wanted to talk to you. He has been admitted to the Medical School."

"Samuil will get in, too," Klara objected and observed, contentedly, that Samuil didn't get distracted from her by the mention of Marik in the same way as he hadn't when he saw her surrounded by the officers. "He just needs to pass chemistry."

As if that were such a small thing! . .

Fira Markovna and Daniil Savvich offered a welcoming smile. In the opposing camp, Strelkina looked proud, Pipa tried being flirtatious, and Volkova sent her a judgmental look.

Rain rapped against the paving stones of the Pavlov Square, the benches of the Gorky Park and the Shevchenko Gardens. Chemistry refused to enter his brain because he was up to his throat in it already. The elevator thundered beneath his foot and yelped behind his back like a dog whose tail he would have gladly stepped on.

Samuil went outside and walked towards the tram station. He realized that tomorrow it was going to be decided whether he would become a doctor. Even if they decided he shouldn't, he was still going to become one, of course.

"What gave you the idea to bring him home?" coldly observed Maria who failed to be surprised by anything at this point. "What could one do for such a long time in the company of this character?"

"We did chemistry, and also I gave him something to eat. Did you see how thin he is? Only people fresh out of a concentration camp are thinner."

"I wouldn't say he's so much thinner as he is scantier," replied Maria in a cold and sarcastic voice. "There is no limit to how much worse one can get but why does he have to be getting worse at our place?"

Klara opened yet another book and said without raising her head,

"Mom, a candidate that is forced upon one can never end up being acceptable. Besides, in contrast to the majority of candidates you found appealing, Samuil is neither klutzy nor schmaltzy. This is a rare quality that, for me, is decisive."

Vladimir Fedorovich was struck by either the expression or the unfamiliar fact of reality. He put down his newspaper and raised his brows with a smile, "What do you mean?"

Klara left aside her book for the moment and explained,

"When such schmaltzy guys talk, their lips flap against each other like a slipper does against a heel."

Maria became silent in an appalled and shaken way, while Vladimir Fedorovich giggled, which provoked a deep indignation on her part. Klara, in the meanwhile, continued her short speech,

"Samuil will be a doctor, and a very famous one, too, Mama, just like you want. He will be just as famous as Marik and Co, which is something we will all see in a few years. By the way, I have nothing against my son being like him. Samuil, I mean."

"Your son?" Maria Isaakovna looked petrified and felt queasier than she used to on board of a military aircraft. It was one thing to stop the fight between Pipa and Volkova, defend a project the likes of which nobody had ever seen, or keep her mouth shut when her teeth chattered against each other in fear. It was, however, a completely different kind of feat to deal with Klara when she seemed to have made a decision of this magnitude.

"What do you mean, a son?" Vladimir Fedorovich was surprised but he had no fear on Klara's behalf. Rather, he was afraid for himself. It was one thing to hold on to the hand of an eight-year-old Klara but an entirely different thing to control Maria's horror and anger.

"I am going to have a son," said Klara and opened her book again.

When she saw that Maria Isaakovna was on the verge of losing consciousness because of her helpless rage mixed with the kind of desperation that was just as helpless and that Vladimir Fedorovich had even stopped smiling, Klara added in a comforting tone,

"I don't think it will happen any time soon, but it will one day."

Then, finally, she could go back to her reading.

XXXV

The sky that was the color of stale chicken seemed to be sniffing with a nose barely covered with clouds. The sun senselessly attempted to break through these clouds. It tried to tear them apart like a drunken worker who twice a month tears the shirt on his own or on his neighbor's chest. One felt like killing somebody, or better yet, everybody, but one felt so gloomy and despondent that even this didn't feel like an option.

"Samuil," Klara enunciated in a merciless way, "your nose is not that aquiline as it is, so if you allow it to get out of joint, it will not look very pretty. It isn't like you, either. So let go of this doom and gloom and let's start thinking about how we can remedy the situation. It makes no sense to lie on a bed of nails, which is why we need to come up with something more productive."

I didn't feel like saying anything in response or doing anything at all. I couldn't avoid saying something to her, though, since she looked at me in a way that felt like she was grabbing me and shaking me.

"I'll live at my parents' place for the moment," he said, trying to repress an irrepressible anger at chemistry and all the chemists and alchemists in the world who have nothing whatsoever to do with medicine but who are very proud of being able to combine two useless acids to create a third one. "They will be happy to hire me at the factory. In a year, I'll get a higher-level certification. . ."

"Fine," Klara interrupted him. "This conversation makes very little sense. "Do you have a coin?"

"What coin?" Samuil interrupted himself.

"To make a phone call. Do you have a 15-copeck coin?"

As good luck might have it, the pay phone was in working order.

"Hi Dad," Klara said into the receiver. "Senia and I are on Sumskaya Street right now, near the Gorky Park. He had his chemistry exam today... No, there is no need to worry, I always speak in this single-minded tone of voice... No, there is no cause for celebration yet... This is exactly what I wanted to ask you... Great, we'll be over in a moment... Dad, you don't need to cook, we are just going to talk business. Besides, I'm sure you have no food in the house... Yes, that's exactly what I needed! What is it that you are planning to celebrate with him, if I may ask?.. Getting to know each other? Well, in that case, I'll try not to object... Hugs, and I'll see you soon."

"Can your Dad help?" Samuil asked without his customary enthusiasm.

Klara flashed her eyes that had darkened in concentration and enunciated, as she headed towards Mayakovskaya Street and led Samuil in the chosen direction,

"In the worst-case scenario, you'll just meet my Dad and celebrate getting to know each other, even though I'm opposed to these banalities. In the best case, we will figure something out together. A group, which I normally dislike, can be very powerful."

The sun had finally managed to tear the shirt on its chest and revealed a blue, freshly laundered undershirt. Sparrows bathed in the dust, laughing noiselessly and flapping their wings.

"This means it is going to rain," concluded Klara contentedly without even suspecting that Samuil and Klara would be walking this very minute – here they come, right there, can't you see them? – down Sumskaya Street and towards the marketplace. In a building right next to the tram stop, in a communal apartment, lived Zinovi Stolberg. Klara couldn't think about her right now, however, because she was concentrated on one thing and one thing only. She had made a decision to remove an obstacle that had appeared on her way, which meant that the poor obstacle was to be pitied.

"Dad, meet Samuil," Klara said. "Senia, this is Zinovi Iosifovich, my father."

"I understand, Klara," Zinovi said, signaling his agreement with Klara's choice. "And as for you, young man, it would be hard not to understand your choice."

"So what's new, sweetheart? How is the dagger doing?"

"Dad gave me a German dagger as a gift," Klara explained. "It's a real one, made of stainless steel – as opposed to this rusty herring you can see on the table."

Zinovi filled his own and Samuil's glass, they downed the alcohol, celebrating getting acquainted, and Zinovi breathed out, "Senia, please tell me what's happening and I'll start thinking about what can be done."

They were eating potatoes baked yesterday or the day before with rust-covered herring that was still almost tasty and rye bread.

"What's happening is simple," Samuil replied. "Unlike chemistry. Since ten people competed for each spot, I had to get an A for the chemistry exam. The problem is that I can get an A for any subject save chemistry and physics. Well, physics is not that bad. But these stupid salts and alkaline solutions and reactions of replacement are impossible to remember, no matter how much I cram. Klara tried helping me study for two whole days but it was all for nothing. Besides, I really hate cramming, to tell you the truth. I can't remember what I don't understand."

"What is it you would like to understand?"

"Why I need to learn it in the first place. Just tell me, Zinovi Iosifovich, how can I pass the exam if I don't see the point of taking it?"

"So as far as I understand, you simply got a low grade," Zinovi concluded. "Emotions aside, am I right?"

"What do you mean, 'simply'?" Samuil almost chocked on the rust. "That's precisely the problem. I got a low grade and will now go work at the factory as a fitter."

"That's not a bad option," Zinovi observed.

"Sure enough, Zinovi Iosifovich. Only I don't want options. I will work as a doctor and then do all the fitting I need after that."

Zinovi thought for a while and observed, "From your story, I can conclude that the people who administered your exam can hardly be accused of not being objective..."

He paused briefly and added, "However, nothing is more subjective than the so-called objective opinion. In your case, as far as I can judge, the decisive factor was subjectivity confused with superlative objectivity..."

Klara frowned and said, "Dad, when did you learn to use a shot-glass with such expertise? Even though it doesn't affect your logical reasoning, Samuil might get a wrong impression about me."

I smiled and was going to reassure them that I had no doubt that she had inherited only the most impeccable traits, but Zinovi laughed and responded, "This is what allowed us to give them a good thrashing. Of course, we had no shot-glasses or many other things with us."

"I had a flask," Samuil nodded.

"Exactly. When it was really cold, each of us would receive not a regular but a soldier's flask with pure alcohol. The flask had a screw-on cap that was as big as a glass. When we were out in the field in freezing cold, we'd never get drunk, no matter how much we'd drink. We just managed to stay warm for a while."

Samuil nodded in agreement as he chewed the last piece of herring. Klara smiled in a way that was similar to Vladimir Fedorovich's when she told him about the tsar and the king.

Zinovi continued,

"Every one of us knew that you breathe in, pour the alcohol into your mouth, swallow, and breathe out immediately. But those guys were useless, no matter how many times you tried explaining it to them. Let me give you an example. This happened during the Battle of Stalingrad, in 1943. It was February, if I'm not mistaken. Once, I saw this POW German who was so covered with grime that he didn't even look blond any more. He'd been frozen solid. I decided to help him because, leaving aside the nasty details, he was still a human being. So I show him how it's done: inhale, swallow, exhale. He nods in agreement, takes the screw-on cap, inhales, downs the alcohol, and swallows."Exhale," I tell him. But he just stands there, his eyes wide open, staring into space, like a crazy person. The other guys gathered around and also yell, "Exhale, you idiot!" And he just stands there and stares. And then, all of a sudden, he just dropped into the snow. We thought he's died."

"So what happened?"

"You won't believe it but he simply fell asleep. He stayed sleeping for one whole day and then came back to life."

There was no more alcohol left to toast this but Zinovi said in the same breath, "You know, we could still do something!"

Dimples came back to Klara's cheeks.

"Dear Zinovi Iosifovich," Samuil exclaimed in a tone of a happy performer of opera arias, "I'll eagerly await your commands. I promise to do exactly as you say!"

"There's nothing for you to do just yet. I will ask somebody I know for advice. There is a chance something can be done. If you didn't care about what happened, then you wouldn't stand a chance. Just ask any doctor. OK, my friends, let's say goodbye now and tomorrow will be a new day. I never understood this expression, but I'm just a regular guy, incapable of understanding such things. Let's get in touch tomorrow."

Klara's dimples, her blush and her eyes laughed. As for Samuil, more than anything, he wanted to start doing something already.

"Klara and I were going to the monument opening tomorrow morning, but if needed, I can just go to Klara's place, and we'll stay there waiting for you to call."

"Go to see the monument, and then tell me about it."

Samuil saw Klara home and crossed the city to reach his parents' house on Dobrokhotova Street. The tram had worked very hard during the day and was now clanging and ringing down the streets and across the river in an unhurried trot because there was no reason for it to hurry. Samuil was looking out of the window at the streets that were saying good-bye to him for the night, at the pavement, at the rain that was the same color as wet cement. In his hands, he held a bag that he had received from Klara and that contained a can of crab meat and a flat white-and-blue package of sugar. Klara demanded that he eat them in his own but how could he do it in the presence of his hungry parents, sister and niece? It wasn't like he was hide behind the house and gobble the food down in secret. He laughed out loud when he imagines this unimaginable scenario.

He felt happy and light, and there was so much time still before tomorrow arrived, and life was so endless that one didn't even think about it...

The three stairs that looked like they were made of marble, the elevator that gave its customary thump with its customary deep bottom and clanged with its customary cast-iron door that was concealed behind the customary wooden panels.

"Sweetheart, you will still have a lot of these sun bunnies in your life," Zinovi told her in a friendly voice that sounded like he was asking for her advice or giving it when she went back for her handbag.

I gave him a kiss and answered without thinking twice, "Dad, I will only have a lot of him. As for others, I hope not to have even a small number of them."

Zinovi hugged her, "Are you so sure already?"

"There are no guarantees, as we all know."

"Well, God be with you. . . I hope you figure it out and discover that there are no hidden dangers."

Klara kissed her mother who was unhappy to see her daughter come home so late. She smiled at Vladimir Fedorovich who was emitting penetrating snores and discovered that she was in luck. Strelkina was away from the bathroom. Of course, she will make up for it tomorrow but that's still so far away in the future. Tomorrow and today are like different eras.

Tomorrow she will have to think about the reasons why today and yesterday are so much alike that they sometimes look like the same thing. . . She will definitely have to think about it but much later. Tomorrow. . .

XXXVI

Sumskaya Street knew very well how to make itself look young. Now it had something to be proud of and it made full use of this opportunity. From this moment on, it was going to have its own Gosprom, albeit a miniature one. A white gazebo that had been erected in front of Shevchenko Gardens looked somewhat like Gosprom's tower. This remote similarity was not the most important thing, though. And neither was the minuscule lake with two floating houses, a lakelet where black and white swans swam, looking pensive and proud. In their condescension, the swans avoided paying attention to the thousands of people who had gathered for the opening of the Glass Fountain.

What would even be the point of paying attention, - the birds who were occupied with other-worldly concerns must have thought, - to those who are so sadly and hopelessly out of touch with refined issues which burden only them. They, the swans, were the bearers of truth that was inaccessible to everybody else. . . Like ancient galleys, they soundlessly and immovably plowed the waters of their swan lake. At times, they would peek into floating houses or come out onto the marble shore in order to stretch their white and black necks in an elegant way, glance distractedly over the multitude of admiring faces, and float away yet again down the endless, minuscule lakelet next to the Glass Fountain.

The people who gathered in the middle of the bombastically playful Sumskaya Street were almost as happy as they had been on that day in May when the stars and the music feel into their hands of their own accord. Of course, they weren't happy in the same way but, still, they were, and the scorching August heat meant nothing to them.

The stream of water coming out of the Glass Fountain itself did not have a single tiny little wrinkle and reminded one of a baby's cheek. It descended from the tower that looked like Gosprom's one and flowed down without stopping, as if it had been stopped in its tracks either by its own beauty or by a reluctance to spoil everybody's pleasure.

"And what if tomorrow it gets freezing cold?" asked Samuil both of Klara and of himself.

"They will probably turn off the fountain in winter," Klara suggested.

"I don't mean the fountain. Of course, you can just turn it off and forget about it. But what about the swans, though? Usually, swans and ducks fly South in winter... Do you think these ones will fly away, too?"

He put his arm around Klara's shoulders as if fearing that she was going to fly away as well. Klara, however, shrugged off his arm (who needs these public displays of passionate affection?) and dispelled his doubts, "Only the wild ones leave. The domesticated birds have to be protected from the cold. The zoo is very close by here, you know? Before the war, I used to take Vladimir Fedorovich there."

She smiled at the look Samuil gave her and explained, "Do you think he'd even go to the zoo if it hadn't been for me?"

"True," Samuil agreed. "There are times when one has to take matters into one's own hands in a way that allows the other person to believe it was his own decision. This might matter to him a lot more than everything else."

Klara smiled, "Neither I nor Vladimir Fedorovich would go to the zoo on our own. I dislike both the zoo and the circus. It smells really bad there, and the animals get tortured to entertain people. To tell you the truth, I loathe being entertained. As if I couldn't entertain myself perfectly well whenever I feel like it. I only went to the zoo for his sake, just as he went there for mine."

"So you both pretended to like it there?" Samuil smiled. "An agreement is the product of both parties' informed consent, right?"

Klara laughed.

"You are a great student. I'm impressed with how well you reproduce the terminology."

"Say, how did you manage to pretend so well when you were just a little kid?" Samuil asked while still laughing.

Klara stopped laughing. She cast a glance around the Sumskaya Street, the Shevchenko Gardens, and then allowed her gaze to return to the Glass Fountain.

"I was very happy. . . It was great to leave the house in the morning, go for walks with Vladimir Fedorovich, and then return home to Mom. Sometimes, we'd meet Dad, although that didn't happen very often. . . All kinds of funny stories kept happening."

She burst out laughing again, "I was worried those times had ended but now it turns out they are still going on."

Samuil sighed.

"So I remind you of Vladimir Fedorovich, right?"

"No," Klara said and shook her raven-black mane of hair. "I haven't yet been able to get Vladimir Fedorovich to quit smoking. With you, though, I managed that in a flash."

Samuil laughed, while Klara stopped smiling and suddenly asked, "Senia, do you agree that no happiness exists, just force of will and peace?"

Samuil didn't need to think twice.

"If a great poet said this, he should know what he's talking about. The greats are who they are in order to know things that we, the lowly ones, can't comprehend. Instead of thinking for oneself, you can just trust the great one's opinion and rest easy."

"And how about free will?"

"Well, it isn't like anybody is forcing you to do anything. You can believe the great one's opinion of your own free will and end up freely resting easy."

"It's easy for you to giggle about this. My mother gave me this book as a gift when I was just eight years old. I was sure that I'd grow up one day and finally realize why "no happiness exists." But here I am, all grown up, and I still don't get it. . ."

"For the peace to substitute happiness, one first needs to get really tired. Otherwise, you can end up believing that the dead are the happiest people around. As you can imagine, a corpse is more at peace than all the rest of us combined. I, however, never felt like I needed to be at peace, even when I'd get tired like a dog in Arkul. I'm doing well enough without any extra peace, thank you very much. There was also a lot of free will, both in Arkul and here. All I need now is to get into Med School, and then I'll be so happy like your Pushkin couldn't even begin to imagine."

"But what if you believe you are happy when, objectively, it isn't so?"

"My love, it makes no sense to try and convince such a person otherwise. Let people enjoy their happiness. If one believes he is happy, that means he truly is happy. Who are we to believe we know better?"

"Samuil Semenovich, you are a subjective idealist."

"Klarissa Zinovievna, I'm rather an ideal subject. Or haven't you noticed that yet."

The respectable Sumskaya Street closed its eyes and stopped its ears for fear that Samuil would whistle through three fingers or even two bended in a circle with the kind of whistle that could make the entire city of Kharkov, from the Forest Park to the Cold Mountain, shudder.

"Still, one can't always be happy."

"Then he's a fool. And whose fault is that?"

"Senia, this is your youthful optimism speaking."

"My love, I'm still too young for old-age optimism!.. I'm not suggesting that one walk around smiling like an idiot all the time. One can be in a really bad mood but if one then gets into a good mood once again, that means he is happy. A bad mood is no obstacle to happiness, unless, of course, you drag it out forever. I think it even has its practical uses when administered in small quantities. It can help one feel grounded in reality. Too much of it, though, can easily put you under the ground. This is my medical opinion."

"It's great that you argue with authorities. I like that."

"What's the point of arguing with the geniuses? It's good to be a genius. You have a nice meal, take a nap, and then wake up and come out with yet another profound pronouncement meant to make you and I think and sigh, "Yes, this is very deep." Maybe you and I should be each other's geniuses instead. You will be mine, and I will be yours. Agreed?"

"Agreed! I loved pretending I was a genius when I was little."

The condescending albeit rejuvenated Sumskaya plunged into the cozy Mayakovskaya Street with a thud of its tramway. Klara pressed the button the required number of times, and Zinovi Stolberg opened the door for them.

XXXVII

"You see?" Petro Antonovich nodded contentedly. "I'm right, as usual. And you, Ziama, sometimes doubt me. You just can't accept that I'm always right."

"What is it that you are right about this time?" said Zinovi to signal his disagreement. "The kid asked you a direct question and, instead of dispelling his legitimate doubts, you are beating around the bush."

"Doubts can't be legitimate," objected Petro Antonovich who was happy with the way the discussion was going. "A person who doubts is wrong by default. I, however, am always right," he said to conclude this complex idea.

Klara had been observing them with a worried look on her face. At this point, she felt obligated to interrupt their academic discussion.

"Dad, you are trying to get this respectable man drunk."

"It's him who's getting me drunk!" Zinovi objected. "Everybody knows they get us drunk and involve us in all kinds of trouble."

"It's the opposite," Petro replied. "You are the ones who get us drunk involve us in trouble. Just wait and see, soon you'll be accused of that, too."

The four of them stayed pensive for a while.

"Petro Antonovich," said Samuil to revive the discussion. "Please explain it to me because I don't get it."

"What is it that you don't get, kid?" Petro Antonovich asked him patiently in Ukrainian, his native language.

"What if everything comes out? What shall we do then?"

"The truth always comes out eventually," Klara agreed.

Petro Antonovich nodded as contentedly as before.

"Yes, Ziama, I told myself – and yourself, too – that the people often make mistakes. Way too often. Even though we keep being told that the people are always right, the truth of the matter is that I'm the one who's always right, not the people."

"That's true," Zinovi nodded. "The people are silent."

"Dad," interrupted Klara yet again. "Stop pouring out the drinks. Both of you will talk yourselves into so much trouble right now that you won't even believe it when you finally wake up."

"I'm not the one who said it first," Zinovi exclaimed.

"True," Petro Antonovich confirmed. "It wasn't him. And the subject under discussion is different. He wouldn't have said something like this."

"Quod licet jovi, non licet bovi," Klara observed in a strict voice. "I'm telling you this as a future lawyer."

"She's all grown up now," said Zinovi with a sigh.

"They keep growing," Petro Antonovich agreed and also let out a sigh.

The two friends and Samuil raised their glasses again and pondered the issue a while longer.

"Just look at what it is that the people are saying," said Petro to continue the conversation.

"What?" Zinovi repeated in an interested and thoughtful way.

The wise men and their young charge ingested some of the contents of the cans spread on the table. Klara didn't eat because she was trying to figure out where the discussion was going. For now, she was failing at this task.

"The people, Ziama," Petro Antonovich said wistfully, "says that you, folks, are persp. . . persp. . .persp. . ."

"Petro Antonovich, please chew your food and stop worrying," Klara suggested with compassion, assuming that he was having a bout of hiccups. "Here, drink some water and stay silent for a moment. Like Vladimir Fedorovich, would say, may the devil take them all, those people. OK, this is better. Now, can you address the issue?"

He wagged his finger while Zinovi nodded his head.

"No, Klarochka," Petro Antonovich smiled. "The issue is very deep."

"It's an important issue, sweetheart," Zinovi nodded sadly, as he realized that there was no more drink to pour out.

"Per. . .spicacious!" Petro Antonovich finally managed to say the key word feeling proud of managing to bring it out in its entirety.

"And what are we in reality?"

"You are just the opposite, like I've been saying. You, folks, can't manage to perspicate anything."

Petro Antonovich stopped eating because there was no more food and even less drink left. He took out a pack of cigarettes and extended it to Zinovi.

"Don't even think about it!" Klara exclaimed and took the pack away. "This isn't the war, my friends. You are now back to the civilian life. Let's finally discuss the issue."

"They keep growing," sighed Petro.

"She's all grown up now," agreed Zinovi and also sighed.

They both pondered the issue wistfully.

XXXVIII

The Vice-Chancellor of the Medical School, Mikhail Petrovich Dragonchuk, wiped the sweat off his brow with a hopelessly wet, useless handkerchief and hung his jacket on the back of his chair. The tiny fan was doing all it could but what could it really achieve in such a scorching heat? It only succeeded in moving the hot air that felt like hot steam around the office and blowing around the fluff from the poplar trees. How it managed to get into his office when the windows were closed remained a mystery.

As usual, there was more work than he could hope to do, and the heat stayed and grew even more oppressive than usual. Well, that was August for you. Instead of calming down before a long Fall and an endless winter, the nature become more cruel than ever. No thermometer could resist its pressure. If a human being reached the kind of temperature that the air both in and outside of the Vice-Chancellor's office had, he would be prescribed. . . What did people get prescribed in such cases? The best remedy, of course, would be hot tea with raspberry jam, even though it was so hot. And staying in bed. Resting and eating well. The best kind of medicine, Mikhail Petrovich decided, was not the kind taught at his Med School but the kind passed down from one's grandmother to one's mother.

Mikhail Petrovich heaved a sad sigh. Wouldn't it be great to rest and eat well right now? But there was so much work that one couldn't even consider staying in bed and eating well. The competition was ten prospective students for each available spot. That was the average, of course. At some departments, the competition was even fiercer. There were too many issues to address and too many tasks to complete. Reports, paperwork, letters, relationships, accounting, figures, letters, words, words, words. . . Where could a single individual find the energy needed to fulfill all these tasks? He wanted to feel sorry for himself but it was so hot that he didn't even have energy for self-pity. . .

God, where do you find energy for everything one needs to accomplish? God, of course, had no idea. The Vice-Chancellor, however, somehow managed it. Because if one failed to do so, one would get into a lot of trouble. So it was easier to stop complaining and just do the work. The good thing was that the war was over because what could be worse than the war? Now we could deal with anything.

Mikhail Petrovich heaved a happier sigh, wiped the sweat off his brow with an even more useless handkerchief, stuck his head in front of the exhausted fan for a while, and started working on yet another document. And then an event took place that even he, a person who had seen all the imaginable and the unimaginable couldn't have conceived of.

It happened as the sun sizzled above Kharkov as a bacon rasher on a frying pan, puffed as a kettle that had been left behind in the communal kitchen and touched the earth with its inflamed forehead even though the ground was mortally tired of its heat. The sun had had enough of its own cruel hot-headedness and was now sick and tired of itself.

Like a conflict-mongering inhabitant of a communal apartment, however, once it had flared up, it couldn't stop and just kept heating, glowing, blazing, and scorching. Maybe it simply couldn't put up with the fact that there were only a few days left before the beginning of the conciliatory Fall and was trying to mark the end of the summer by making a weighty statement. Probably the sun wanted to get the people and the streets that were exhausted by the heat wave to remember it for a long time to come, until next summer came around.

The poplars on Lenin Avenue faded and drooped and their grey fluff was flying around with complete and utter impunity. It penetrated through the closed, fogged up windows of spacious buildings in one of which Mikhail Petrovich Dragonchuk was signing yet another document. This time it was the list of students who had been accepted to the Med School.

Before Mikhail Petrovich had time to get to the letter "T", the securely closed door of the Vice-Chancellor's office flew open. It did so in such an impetuous manner that one could have said it shot open rather than flew open. Right in front of him, Mikhail Petrovich saw a sergeant who was offering him a happy but reserved smile. The soldier was wearing military boots, jodhpurs and a soldier's blouse that had two dozen of combat medals pinned on it. If only that were all, though! The most striking thing was that all these medals paled in comparison with one of them, namely, the soldier's Hero Star.

"Good afternoon, Comrade Vice-Chancellor!" the sergeant said with a jocular seriousness and offered his hand for Mikhail Petrovich to shake.

The Vice-Chancellor looked like his tongue had suddenly gotten numb.

"Klara and Samuil must have felt just like this the night before, when we first met at Zinovi Stolberg's place," Petro Antonovich mused. It was funny but flattering. Most importantly, it was often useful.

"Sergeant Kosachenko," introduced himself Petro Antonovich in a firm and loud voice as he shook the Vice-Chancellor's hand and smiled – both at him and at his own thoughts.

During the evacuation Mikhail Petrovich had worked in a military hospital. There, he spent over two years cutting and sewing heroes and anti-heroes, the recipients of all possible medals, and pre-war award winners who during the war became regular soldiers and officers. He never knew how many of them he attended, whether there were hundreds or thousands. Neither then nor now did he have time to consider that. Mikhail Petrovich himself had quite a few medals for a doctor. One thing, however, he could have never imagined in his wildest dreams: that one day he would have his hand shaken by a Hero of the Soviet Union.

Mikhail Petrovich got up from his chair, failing to locate the tongue that had strayed to an unidentified location inside his mouth, turned off the annoying fan, put on his jacket, wiped his wet forehead with an even wetter handkerchief, and, having finally found his tongue, replied,

"Please be seated, Comrade Hero of the Soviet Union."

"So what is this that I hear?" Petro Antonovich offered an even more serious smile as he sat down, facing the Vice-Chancellor in a chair that was too fragile for his bulk. "How come such a serious institution mistreats an orphan?"

In the side pocket of his jacket, Mikhail Petrovich palpated his Communist Party membership card with a sweaty palm. He almost handed it over to the sergeant in recognition of not being fit to own it but stopped himself in time, sat down into his chair and dared to object.

"That cannot be true, Comrade Hero of the Soviet Union. There must be some misunderstanding . . . or you might have been misinformed. We couldn't have mistreated an orphan."

Petro Antonovich's severe smile was transformed into one that was almost paternal. He offered the Vice-Chancellor a cigarette, lit one for himself, extended the lighter to Mikhail Petrovich and continued,

"You see, I just got demobilized and came back to my native city. Yesterday, I saw my nephew, and he's sad, miserable, just completely down and out."

"Is there something I can do to help?" Mikhail Petrovich asked feeling relieved and compassionate.

"You are actually the only one who can help," Petro Antonovich confirmed. "Senia is a great guy. He just graduated from a vocational school and can do anything with his hands. For as long as he's lived, he's dreamt of becoming a doctor. He applied to your Medical School but didn't get in because of losing just a couple points at the entrance exams."

At this time, Mikhail Petrovich felt so relaxed that he didn't even notice the heat any more. He smoked and listened to the sergeant with a calm sense of enjoyment.

"The guy has no parents. He's an orphan. In the evacuation, he lugged sacks of flour from the mill to the factory since he was fifteen years old. He had to look out for himself because there wasn't anybody to take care of him. This is one heroic boy who's all alone in the world."

Petro Antonovich took a drag out of his cigarette and concluded his story, "Are we going to deprive our country of a great doctor just because of a couple of silly points? Are we just going to give up on the guy? It isn't like you are some kind of a bureaucrat, comrade Vice-Chancellor. Or are you?"

XXXIX

With a heavy and helpless gait, the sun walked over the horizon that was concealed from view by high, almost high-rise, buildings. It was so tired that it didn't even cast a glance through the iron-hot windows of the city. The poplar fluff that was still sleepily descending onto the soft asphalt on Lenin Avenue was the only reminder of the red-hot, sizzling rasher.

"Petro Antonovich, seriously," Samuil repeated insistently. "How can I pass for an orphan? What if it all comes out? Then nobody will accept me anywhere at all. And that's the least serious of the possible consequences."

"Besides," Klara observed in a judicious manner, "how come somebody who bears a very Ukrainian name of Petro Antonovich Kosachenko suddenly ended up with a nephew called Samuil Semenovich Blekhman, which is as Jewish as one can get?"

Zinovi and Petro sighed because there was no food and drink left and stared at each other pensively.

"The younger generation is really great, Ziama," said Petro in a sentimental voice.

Zinovi wistfully agreed,

"We will be able to leave the world in really good hands, Petro."

Klara grabbed a big white apple out of the vase, took a bite out of it, and thought that the two buddies weren't even remotely likely to leave the world just yet. They looked less like the wise old sages who were preparing to give way to the younger generation than like characters from popular movies about young friends who were heroic and funny at the same time. She didn't feel like going outside at all because she felt so calm and secure at home. The clock was ticking, and each tick reminded her of water drops falling in a way that was both happy and a little sleepy at the same time.

Klara peeked into her father's work room. He was finishing a very unusual wardrobe that had been ordered last Tuesday or thereabouts. Here Dad is touching up the right-hand door of the wardrobe with a small brush. Here he is, at this very moment. The wardrobe is the color of black cherries. Or is it dark brown? A deeply respected wardrobe, isn't it? It's brand-new, heavy and as reliable as their entire house, their entire life which – even though Klara doesn't even stop to think of it – will last forever. It will last forever because . . . well, how else can it be? It doesn't even make sense to think about that. Here Dad is turning towards her. . . no, first he sniffles in his funny way, just like he always does. And how great it is that he always does it! And now, right at this very moment, right now, yes, right this second, he turns towards her, leaves his brush on the small table, smiles – here he is, smiling, just like he always does, always! – and says, "Sweetheart, there is nothing better than today."

Klara smiled or felt sad; she couldn't have told the difference between these two at this point. She looked past Zinovi into the window that had already concealed Samuil. Hail beat against the window-sill with the same sound as Mom's necklace would have done if broken, so how was one supposed to go visit the Krupetskys? Klara felt sad and smiled at the same time and said, as she was looking out of the window,

> We kept telling the present to move ahead,
> But we suddenly felt the breath of cold.
> Turning back, we saw the past in our stead
> For our life story had already been told.

"The present continues but the past, unfortunately, does not," Klara smiled sadly. "Dad, let's live for today, no matter what today is like. Especially since it's always good, even when it's bad."

"This sounds very convincing," Zinovi nodded. "As I can hear, you have disinterred a new writer."

"This poem was written by Vladimir Benediktov, Dad."

Zinovi shook his head because he couldn't remember the name.

"It must be a classical author, right? Judging by the style and the rhyme?"

"He didn't manage to become a classic, even though he was as famous as Pushkin, especially at poetic gatherings in respectful houses. Benediktov was wistful like Samuil after his chemistry exam. Samuil got over it fast, though, while Vladimir Benediktov never did."

Zinovi sat on the sofa next to Klara.

"Vladimir Benediktov didn't have Klara because if he did, his blues would be over pretty soon, too. Where did you find this Benediktov?"

"At the Korolenko library. It's a very good, two-volume edition, old, from 1909."

Zinovi smiled, "It's your mother's year. Maria was born in 1909. . . And you were born exactly twenty years later."

Maria, in the meanwhile, regaled Samuil with a severe look that was as old as creation itself. She looked down on him, even though he was much taller than her and never hunched his shoulders, and enunciated,

"Hallo, Samuil. Your face looks just like a moldy potato today."

Samuil had no time to address her gift. He was on his way to the Med School and, as he walked, he was mentally preparing for his conversation with the Vice-Chancellor. This was going to be the most important conversation of his life after the one he'd had in the square next to the Law School.

"My greetings, Maria Isaakovna!" he flashed his eyes and almost sang out with a fierce tenor that sounded like a telegram, "I'm sorry; I have an appointment with Professor Dragonchuk. I'm being accepted into Med School. Give my regards to Vladimir Fedorovich!"

Maria gave him a burning look and headed towards her golden Engineering House. She was thinking that Samuil hadn't sent his regards to Klara, and, unfortunately, it wasn't simply a sign of his bad manners.

XL

The Vice-Chancellor looked at the nephew attentively. The guy reminded him of the uncle in a way that was hard to define. Mikhail Petrovich turned off the fan and opened the window. Yesterday's heat was long gone. The sun had given up on everything and hid behind a grey and purple curtain. A breath of fresh air came from the direction of Gosprom and announced a shower or maybe even hail.

The nephew stood at attention, flashing his eyes and smiling brightly. He was incredibly skinny and wore even more incredibly flared pants and a shirt with a wide collar. He had black, slicked back hair and hands with long, thin fingers.

"Sit down, Senia," Mikhail Petrovich smiled at him and shook his surgeon's or, in the worst of cases, pianist's hand.

"Thank you, Mikhail Petrovich," Samuil responded in a loud voice, and it seemed to Mikhail Petrovich that he was about to emit a whistle that would make the window-panes in the Vice-Chancellor's office rattle. "Don't worry; I will not let you down!"

The Vice-Chancellor smiled once again, "You don't even know yet what it is that I want to offer you."

"It isn't like you'll offer anything bad! Mikhail Petrovich, please, you can rely on me like you can rely on yourself."

"Sounds convincing," Mikhail Petrovich nodded and closed the window.

Minuscule hail stones had started to tap on the windowsill. The Vice-Chancellor returned to his arm-chair.

The hail that was both harsh and funny at the same time turned into an overwhelming shower that huffed and puffed over Kharkov until it finally splashed into the countless puddles with its last drops. The drops were heavy, tired, and worn out after the rumbling shower. Klara smiled as she thought that they had run out of energy to stay hanging in the skies and that was why they fell onto the empty asphalt of the Sumskaya Street, feeling exhausted and relieved.

"It rained and rained for such a long time, but now all that remains of it could have been cried by a cat," Klara smiled as she looked out of the window. Zinovi smiled too when he looked at Klara.

"I've been accepted as an auditing student!" a soaked through Samuil burst in on the highest note of a non-existent musical scale.

"You'll get Dad all wet!" Klara exclaimed, peeling him off Zinovi. "Dad, give him something warm and dry. But no spirits."

XLI

A regular student should come to all classes not because he can't imagine his life without this particular class (why shouldn't he imagine his life without it, actually?) but simply because if he skips it, he will be expelled from college. Then, he will be drafted into the army and will have to apply all over again and start attending all classes or face another expulsion.

An auditing student, however, is free to audit or not, that's all up to him. Samuil hated taking orders from anybody but, in this case, nobody tried ordering him about. The most important thing was that he had finally been accepted, even though just as an auditing student, to the Medical School.

"You'll audit during the Fall semester, then you will pass the finals," Mikhail Petrovich explained to him in a fatherly voice he used with orphans. "Will you pass the finals?"

"How can I possibly avoid passing them?" Samuil exclaimed in the voice of an opera singer preparing for his first triumphant tour across the endless stretches of his homeland.

Truth be told, Mikhail Petrovich didn't doubt him but he had to ask because he was Vice-Chancellor first and a father figure second.

"Then start attending classes," he continued, "pass the finals, and as soon as one of our mamma's boys and papa's girls drops out, I will give you a full-time student status. Don't you worry, some of them will drop out for sure. Studying to be a doctor isn't all that much easier than working as a doctor. And working as a doctor is quite hard, I know that for sure."

"It doesn't matter, Mikhail Petrovich. It's always better to be a doctor than a patient!" Samuil said to dispel his doubts, smiling like an opera singer accepting the applause of his enraptured audience.

"That's true. Do you have a place to stay? If not, you can sleep at school, on the desks. Or the professor's table. It's hard but you'll be completely free, and no noisy neighbor will trouble you. Just like at the cemetery. Will that work for you?"

Samuil hugged Mikhail Petrovich and slapped his shoulder.

"Mikhail Petrovich, my dear friend, of only everybody in the world was like you, I don't even know what would happen. . . God help you!"

The Vice-Chancellor smiled, "Thank you. Just try not to slap everybody's shoulders, Senia, because people might not like that."

"Mikhail Petrovich, I do it out of love!" Samuil exclaimed happily, still looking like an opera singer blowing a kiss to his grateful listeners.

The Vice-Chancellor wrote something on an official form, glanced out of the window on the beautiful and fashionable avenue, smiled, and concluded, "My experience tells me that not everybody wants to be loved. Many people want the exact opposite."

Samuil emerged onto Lenin Avenue. It was cold and impassive and in no way reminded one of Arkul road with its forefingers of trees whose crows tried to prophesy that his main wish would never come true. Now his wish had come true, no matter how much these black monsters cawed. Recently, however, he began to wish for something else, which was no less – and possibly even more – important.

Samuil burst out with happy laughter and whistled so loudly that the inoffensive Kharkov swallows lost even the puny powers of speech that the nature, always stingy with its gifts, awarded them at birth. The passers-by turned away in muted indignation, thinking that one couldn't take a step without meeting a syavka. Not only did this guy wear pants with a huge flare and a shirt that was open on his chest, he also whistled like a total syavka, with his pinky finger. A street is a street, no matter what you say...

"Senia, you can always stay at my place," Zinovi suggested. "And come next semester, you will be offered a dorm room. You will be a full-time student by then, and full-time students are entitled to stay in a dorm."

"No, Zinovi Iosifovich, my friend," Samuil objected decisively. "You have to think of your personal life. I can't stand in the way of that."

"And what about your parents' place?" Petro Antonovich asked. "Of course, it's a long commute to make every single day, but it's your home. It isn't like you are really an orphan."

"That's an important thought, Petro Antonovich," Klara stated. In order not to be an orphan, it isn't enough for one to have parents. It's important that they have one, too."

Stolberg and Kosachenko sighed, raised their glasses, and drank.

"They keep growing," Petro said, chewing sadly on his food.

"They are all grown up now," agreed Zinovi even more sadly and, therefore, taking a bigger mouthful of food.

XLII

Audiatur et altera pars.

The white elephants in the cupboard looked made out of ivory. Klara, however, could only suspect what they were really made of. Now, however, as she listened to Professor Fuks's lecture in an auditorium that was so filled with people that an apple would sooner shrivel with old age on a bough before finding a spot to drop on the floor, she realized that Latin and Latin only possessed the true white hue of ivory and its profound, unshakeable soundness. Latin sentences were imperially impassive and regal. Only a person capable of a slow, careful and respectful learning could hope to master them. They demanded – in a way that was both contemptuous and reserved – a grateful worshipping and a sense of profound inner peace. They were eternal and, as a result, eternally fresh. Klara understood that eternity wasn't at all old, like many people seemed to think. Even though it had begun a very long time ago, eternity was eternally young because who knows when it shall end? Maybe it won't end at all.

The Latin words made ivory reminded her of marble columns. Each one was equally magnificent and equally necessary to ensure that the vault of the regal Latin phrase never came to crumble. These phrases allowed for no interference with their eternal form and content. Not a microscopic change, nor a minuscule frivolity, and not even a tiny bit of interpretation.

Interpretation?

What kind of law is it, - the Latin phrases were ringing out, hanging low over the students' desks that descended as if in the amphitheatre down to Professor Fuks's feet, - what kind of law is it that allows for an interpretation? A law that allows for an interpretation is not a law. It is nothing but a charade that exists for the entertainment not even of the people but of the crowd. A law can only be studied and should only be obeyed. A law is a demanding privilege of the emperor's. An analysis or an interpretation of the law is an effort of the hoi polloi. Not of the people, no. The people are as great or as lowly as their emperor. It turns into hoi polloi together with an emperor who is a representative of the hoi polloi. Who knows which comes first, really?

The Latin phrases didn't lend themselves to translation. Their form could not be separated from their content, while the content was inseparable from the form. This was exactly what Klara had expected and what she had found in the white palace of the Law School built by Beketov in the Roman style and that reminded her of an ivory tower. For her, the "what" and the "how" were inseparable, like the two sides of the gold medal she got when she graduated from high school.

Audiatur et altera pars.

This sentence, smooth and shiny like a gladiator's sword, rang out in the auditorium and clinked like an echo of the powerful, immortal and eternal Roman law. "The other side", that's precisely where Klara wanted to belong. Two sides. One is crushing everything it encounters like a trained hand of a Roman warrior. It assaults you, attacks you, and defeats you with the strength of its iron-clad arguments and its preponderance of proof. The other side is its eternal rival. It is graceful but unbending, flexible but invincibly hard. It responds to every blow with one that is even more precise, to each jab with one that is even more painful, to each argument with one that is even more direct and impossible to deflect.

These two sides cannot exist or even be conceived as existing without each other. This happens because, Professor Fuks continued, if one of them disappears, the other side will be rendered useless. It will lose all meaning, and the law will be substituted by lawlessness.

"There should be only one side!" a plebeian emperor tells his admiring and silent plebeians. "The other side always causes chaos, and chaos is the cause of all ills."

"Let's listen to the other side!" the Roman law demands from the great emperor and his citizens who no longer want to be silent. Its ivory phrases ring out and drown the plebeian squeaks. Klara was, perceived herself to be, this other side. She knew that chaos only exists when there is just one side. There cannot be a two-sided chaos. The only thing that is two-sided is precisely the opposite of chaos. And that is the eternal Roman law.

As she listened do Professor Fuks, Klara dreamt of being accepted among those who made this altera pars of the chosen ones, the privileged other side. She saw herself as the only person capable of carrying on with the cause of the famous Moscow attorney Fedor Plevako. Things weren't going to be any easier for her than they had been for him. But who could be attracted by easiness, anyways? Yes, facing the two judge's assistants of the Soviet court was different from arguing your case in front of a dozen jurors of the tsarist court. Still, somebody who could convince one person would be able to convince all of them.

No matter how much the prosecutor pontificates, no matter how much of his self-righteous anger he pours over the guilty and the innocent, no matter how hard he and his assistant might try, how will they be able to defeat Klara? After the great "Audiatur et altera pars!" rings out, how can she fail to find the words that will save the people who had lost all hope: a drunken priest who spent the money of his parish on a drunken binge, an old woman who stole a tea-pot from the store, a tea pot that costs thirty coins which are still not the thirty silver coins of Judas, a burned-out poet who had given all the promise he ever could and who stopped giving any promise at all?

This was the same poet who wrote an unexpectedly mean, quite Aesopian epigram addressed to some high-ranking individual, for which crime this same high-ranking individual put him on the defendant's bench. As unexpected as the epigram was, it was even more unexpected that the high-ranking individual actually understood the poem published in a popular rag and interpreted it correctly as a personal insult. Klara would accept the challenge of the prosecutor who would look very funny in his righteous anger. For her, it would be child's play to win this unequal (for the prosecutor and all his aides) duel.

"Today," she will say with a kind of smile that the prosecutor and Co will feel like tiny little fishes burning on a hellish frying-pan and will immediately recognize the impossibility and the uselessness of competing with her in terms of logic and eloquence.

"Today, as usual, I turned the corner on Sumskaya Street and suddenly saw that the neighbors' first-grader was drawing a donkey on the pavement with a piece of chalk."

In order to show his complete neutrality, the judge will cover his face with his palm to conceal a beaming smile from the audience. The judge's assistants, that is, the jurors, will not resist the temptation to smile while staring at the prosecutors who will be sweating profusely.

"So let us imagine," Klara will continue with steely heartlessness, "just imagine that I have stopped to take a look at this creation of the neighbors' spawn. Having strained my diseased imagination to its utmost capacity I then turned to the police officer standing nearby and demanded that he place under arrest this youthful offender of His Majesty the Emperor."

At this point, the high-ranking individual will start either to hiccup or to snort, and the spectators will fail to see him as all that high any more.

"'Excuse me, ma'am,' the police officer will protest. "This is absolutely not His Majesty the Emperor, but rather, and please excuse the language that is unfit for a lady's ears, it is an ass!"

"Exactly," I will say being of completely sound mind. "This is precisely what it is, an ass. Don't you observe any offensive likeness here?"

The judge and the jurors will stop controlling themselves and covering their faces with their hands. Even the miserable defendant will smile modestly, feeling a lot less miserable but, actually, quite happy and in little need of being defended. Only the high-ranking individual (or probably even the extremely high-ranking individual), who will at this moment be abandoned even by the prosecutor, will feel sad and lonely and will want to start gnashing his teeth. His helpless snorting will become audible outside of the courthouse, as far as the Nikolaevskaya Square.

"So are you suggesting," will the policeman ask with his eyes rolling out, "that our emperor. . . our emperor. . ."

Klara will smile and, looking at the sorry formerly high-ranking individual who has finished snorting for good and has started hiccupping silently, she will deal him her last, decisive blow.

"'No, my friend,' I will reassure the irate police officer. 'As for me, I don't want to say anything as silly as this. The problem is, though, that I know one seemingly respectable high-ranking individual who suffers from a pernicious habit of finding non-existent connections and analogies that are as dangerous as they are bizarre. At first, this high-ranking individual finds a connection between his own self and some innocent rhyme that has absolutely no relation whatsoever to him. He does it simply because, for some unfathomable reason, he decided to see himself alluded to buy it. Then, he sees His Majesty the

Emperor in what is, I insist, nothing but an ass. If we are to allow our high-ranking individual to continue with his low-ranking elucubrations, he might even end up discovering our Lord and Savior at the bottom of his vodka glass."

Sic transit gloria mundi! These words will ring out in the ears of the miserable, exhausted general. He will feel like an insignificant clerk who has had the misfortune of sneezing at the bald pate of a superior. Then, he will wish for nothing more than being able to scamper away as fast as possible to prevent this bombastic attorney from assaulting him even further with her piercing, bone-crushing statements. The twelve jurors, the two judge's assistants, the judge and even the prosecutor and his aide will burst out in a bout of unashamed, lethal laughter and will applaud her. The sly scribe would weep from the unexpected happiness.

"Bravo, Ms. Stolberg," the famous attorney Plevako says to her with a smile.

"Thank you, colleague," Klara responds, smiling calmly.

And then she whispers into the poet's ear so that the judge who has just announced a verdict of "not guilty" wouldn't hear her words, "And in the future, if you again decide to create this kind of asinine rhyme, remember that neither I nor Plevako will be able to help you."

No, what she really says is,

"Neither Plevako nor even I will be able to help you."

And then, once again, the eternal warning will ring out mercilessly and contemptuously:

Sic transit gloria mundi!

The ivory-colored sky will frown with each of its clouds and then it will become clear that these are not regular clouds, like some people would like to believe, but hopeless bruise-like storm clouds which are about to crash into each other and will erupt in thunders and flashes of lightning. Will this warning be heeded by the miserable poet who suddenly felt happy and the formerly blessed general who suddenly saw himself not as a high-ranking individual but an obvious nobody?

Of course, professor Fuks and the lawyer Plevako and the future lawyer Klara Stolberg will heed it, which is why their earthly glory will never end.

XLIII

"Come in, Samuil," Vladimir Fedorovich let Samuil into the apartment and they shook hands. Pipa was passing by at that moment and she cast her old acquaintance an interested half-glance. Fira Markovna waved her hand at him from the kitchen and Daniil Savvich gave him a wink. Strelkina and Volkova were not there. If they had been, they would have reddened with envy and started to sulk.

"How is school?" Maria Isaakovna asked, looking in the opposite direction. "Are you still auditing?"

"Mama," Klara interrupted in a calm voice, "Samuil has been a regular student for over two years, just like your Marik or Boria Come-out-of-the-sea."

Boria was known to Klara as a guy whose mother took them to the Crimea beach almost until the age when he received his passport. She would sit in the shade and whenever Boria stayed in the water longer than she found acceptable, she called out to him in a loud voice, "Boria! Come out of the sea!"

She would hiss whenever she had to pronounce the "s" sound so much that the sea would get terrified and come out onto the beach even before Boria did to avoid annoying Boria's Mom.

"I wouldn't say I'm just like them," Samuil objected in his joyous opera voice. "I'm much better in all respects."

Maria Isaakovna raised her brows almost sky-high, trying not to imagine which respects this Arkul and Balashovka boy had in mind. Klara, as always, tried to clarify things for her.

"Mama," she observed in a judicious tone, "not everything has been explored yet, which means that the expression 'all respects' should be interpreted like an advance for a distant future. Unless you decide to insist otherwise. I hope, however, that your influence over your only daughter doesn't go that far. Am I right?"

"Dinner is ready!" Vladimir Fedorovich, who was still smiling kindly, decided to lighten up the impossible to lighten mood. Maria Isaakovna again looked in the opposite direction and said, "We haven't had dinner yet. Klara will eat and be ready for you in half an hour."

Samuil waved his hand in a hopeless gesture.

"Klara, I will go take a walk and we'll meet next to the monument to Shevchenko, all right?"

Klara, who, in this situation, felt like she was on both sides simultaneously, avoided entering into an aimless discussion.

"A person who can resist a plate of my rassolnik hasn't been born yet."

"True!" Samuil laughed. "I have already been born! And everything I need to be truly happy is a plate of real rassolnik and your pleasant company."

Klara's rassolnik was more than real: barley and bits of pickled cucumbers created the kind of flavor that no tongue could describe making one want to swallow the tongue in question. The tongues Samuil spoke were sufficient to let him express his admiration of any other dish, be it an appetizer, an entrée, or a dessert. Rassolnik, however, was unique in that it required the kind of epithets and even the kind of verbs that neither Russian nor Ukrainian, nor Yiddish, nor Latin, nor even the not-quite-forgotten German and Latvian possessed. This wasn't only because Samuil, like any regular student, was perennially hungry but, for the most part, because

Klara's rassolnik surpassed all the unimaginable (let alone the imaginable) standards. Even if Samuil happened not to be hungry (Samuil not hungry?), he would still swallow his tongue time and again as he loudly slurped the rassolnik from a yellow wooden spoon painted with red and black flowers.

Having consumed half of his plate of rassolnik and feeling enough inner strength, Samuil announced, "Maria Isaakovna and Vladimir Fedorovich, I want to inform you that I am planning to ask you to allow Klara to become my wife."

Like Petro Antonovich would say, the room was plunged into a scary silence. Vladimir Fedorovich bent even lower over his plate but Maria Isaakovna told him as usual, "Volodia, don't hunch, eat like you are supposed to!" Even though she had expected Samuil to say what he did for several years now, she still was unprepared to hear them. Klara was both incredibly happy and a little scared, in spite of the fact that such requests had no importance for her. She had already said yes to Samuil and this was not even the most important answer, but simply the only one that mattered at all. With a slight mix of dread and curiosity, she listened to the conversation, fearful of imagining what was about to happen.

In the meanwhile, the silence continued.

Since he had decided to start a dinner conversation, Samuil expatiated on his idea that was rich both in meaning and in consequences, "Klara and I will go to the Crimea this summer for our honeymoon."

Crimea had just occurred to him. Nothing was worse than silence, which is why this thought came to him to save the situation. Somebody somewhere had decided that silence is supposed to signify acquiescence and that it is altogether golden. This platitude had become an aphorism but Samuil suspected – or, actually, firmly believed – that it was simply silly. If a person agrees he doesn't stay silent. Rather, he laughs, cries, whispers, screams in glee, whatever one chooses to do and based on how much one agrees. A person remains silent only if he or she is afraid of breaking the silence or doesn't feel like dignifying what is being said with an answer. Besides, as a doctor (or almost a doctor), Samuil knew that it was always better to talk things over than to keep silent. This is why he repeated in order to prevent the pause from continuing and looking at those present in an innocent and questioning manner, "So, as I said, Klara and I are going to the Crimea for our honeymoon. Audiatur now et altera pars."

If the very first phrase had been predictable and not quite informative, now Klara smiled and plunged into pleasant expectation. Vladimir Fedorovich opened his mouth to discuss, at length, the details of both these pieces of welcome news but at that very moment, he realized that what had reigned in the room before that moment wasn't silence but simply an absence of noise. Silence itself had only occurred – yes, it actually occurred – at that moment. In the kitchen, water started to leak from the faucet in anxious and spasmodic droplets. Downstairs, on Sumskaya Street, trolley polls barked and fell off. All seven elephants in the cupboard wiggled their trunks and tails. Klara felt like clouds had gathered in their room and this made even the ivory bust in the bookcase change its appearance and turn a severe grey color instead of snow-white.

"A decent young lady," Maria Isaakovna responded as she disrupted almost noiselessly this terrifying silence that had enveloped them with words that sounded like a verdict of a military tribunal, "a decent young lady will never travel God knows where with God knows whom."

The remaining rassolnik sizzled under Samuil's enraged glare. Vladimir Fedorovich failed to produce a smile, which was something that had never happened to him before, not even in the Ural Mountains after sixteen hours of uninterrupted hard labor in freezing temperatures. Only Klara shrugged her shoulders and smiled on everybody else's behalf.

"You are absolutely right, Mama. Right now, Senia and I will go out for a walk and we will clarify where exactly we are going to make sure we don't end up God knows where. So, how about it, my dear God Knows Whom, are you now ready to take a romantic walk around the favorite places of your future spouse?"

Samuil, who at this point reminded Vladimir Fedorovich and Klara of the dead swells from Vladimir Fedorovich's old story, jumped to his feet, like Klara and Mila would have done to strike a soaring volleyball, and saluted, "For this, I am always ready!"

Then, he added at the top of his voice but without a slightest threat, just as a foregone conclusion for all of the parties present, "I will see you soon!"

Maria Isaakovna left for the kitchen judiciously but coldly and finished the conversation with the most neutral statement possible at that moment, "A fool in a great hurry drinks tea with a fork."

Samuil kissed Klara above one of her dimples and said to Maria Isaakovna's back, "Everything will be fine. I will not drink with a fork and will not forget anything important. Omnia mea mecum porto."

Vladimir Fedorovich nodded his head to show compassion, said "Oh, God", sighed, and sat town in his arm-chair to read the newspaper.

XLIV

The lights gradually turned red. Sumskaya Street slowly receded away from Klara and Samuil towards Gorky Park, while they tried to prevent it from leaving it as slowly by walking down to street to Shevchenko Gardens.

"Why did you say you carry with you all that's yours?" Klara asked Samuil in a voice that was half-joking and half-sad and slipped her arm under his. "Is it because you are poor or because you are cheap?"

"Because I'm generous," Samuil said and kissed her again. "I never put anything off."

"What a lack of foresight," Klara smiled. "Like Mila's aunt Basia would say, "Klarochka, az och und vey, why did you get involved with this guy?" She's also say, "Mulia, when you say the words altera pars, they sound like alter yid. Are you sure that we were also responsible for inventing the Roman law?"

"Does Mila write to you" Samuil hugged her. "How is she doing?"

Klara looked away, across the Salamander House, Tevelev Square and an unseen suburb of Kharkov where they hadn't yet walked.

"Sometimes she writes. . . I also sometimes write to her. . ."

Samuil didn't interrupt and let her finish.

"Time has turned out to be more than hours, days, and all other weeks. For the most part, time is people. This is why I agree with you, Senia, let's carry all that is ours with us."

"And who is this Boria character?" Samuil asked not out of jealousy because there was no reason to be jealous but just to change the topic. "Is he a worthy fellow?"

Klara snickered,

"He is a chap of rare intelligence. Or, rather, he is rarely intelligent. As we used to say at school, he has a houseful of smarts, but the keys to that house have been misplaced. . . Citizen Blekhman, wouldn't you agree that kissing on a bench that is in public view is the utmost in indecency? I don't think people will miss not witnessing the entire depth of our feelings. Please put your hand in a place that represents no danger to you and allow people to guess rather than see everything with their own eyes."

Samuil laughed without bitterness, "Klarochka, you keep me in the darkest misery."

"Your misery isn't all that dark," Klara responded in a judicious voice. "In any case, a luminous personality like yours can look quite piquant if some darkness is added. Let's rather talk about the issue at hand."

"You can ask me anything you want and I'll be happy to reply."

Klara took her hand away from his and said with sarcasm, "Don't beat around the bush, my dear. Marriage is a serious issue. What is this about a spontaneous trim of God knows whom God knows where and even God knows with whom? Samuil, tell me, why did you have to provoke the Etna volcano into erupting?"

"Etna erupted on her own," Samuil said and shrugged his shoulders. "Your Etna, my love, likes nothing more than erupting quantum satis."

"She has been not only mine but also yours for a while now, my dear. Let's both partake of this inevitable joy equally. So where is it that we are going to travel, in case I do agree to it for whatever reason?"

Samuil offered a mysterious smile.

"Sweetie, you can't even imagine how beautiful the place is. Kharkov cannot possibly compare. Especially since, as you say, all we have over here in summer is dust, dirt, mosquitoes, and flies."

"You are right, I can't even begin to imagine," Klara smiled. "Besides, I can't imagine how you can possibly know if the Crimea is beautiful or just the opposite. When did you manage to spend any time there? Have you made any secret trips that you forgot to mention to me?"

Samuil retorted in the same mysterious manner, "Before undertaking anything, one has to imagine it as well as one can."

"And what if the result disappoints you?" Klara asked after thinking it over for a couple of seconds.

"My love, if a person has a goal and envisions really well how it should turn out, there will never be any disappointments. Of course, if you only vaguely know what it is you want, then who's to blame? It's your own fault if the outcome disappoints you."

Klara mused for a while longer as she looked inattentively at the red, dense lights of the passing cars and the rare flashes of cigarettes.

"Sometimes, you keep imagining something," she said, "but it turns out to be completely different in reality. . . Who knows what's better, to hope and be disappointed or to never have any hope at all? Maybe in order to avoid disillusionment, one should never have any illusions to begin with?"

Samuil laughed and gave her a kiss.

"If we abandon all hope, life will inevitably become disappointing. What you and I should do is keep hoping and imagining things that cannot even begin to be imagined. Then, it will all come true and life will be even better than what we could have possibly dreamed of."

Klara considered this for a long time, as if expecting a sailor to come to her help and assist her in getting out of the

Dnieper River. Then, she inhaled deeper and said firmly to the sailor who had arrived just in time, "You are right, my dear God Knows Whom. Getting disappointed is a very tedious enterprise. You and I don't want to feel bored and we will not. And we will also never get disillusioned not because we never had any illusions but, rather, because our illusions will be so powerful that nothing will manage to destroy them."

Darkness descended upon the city of Kharkov. Sumskaya Street had become tired of running here and there and decided to take a nap on a bench under a huge oak tree where Klara and Samuil couldn't be seen any longer. . .

XLV

"Dad, why don't you give me any advice?" Klara asked, showing no surprise.

"What kind of advice can I give you, Klarochka?" responded Zinovi. "Maybe only to hold yourself together. But, first of all, you have somebody to do that for you, and his hands can keep you together better than either you or I could. Also, in order to fail at holding yourself together, you don't really need to travel outside of Kharkov. How is your mother doing? How is Vladimir Fedorovich?"

"Mother has gone to Lake Balkhash. Vladimir Fedorovich sends his greetings. Dad, it smells of perfume here, and that perfume is not mine."

Zinovi gave a sigh of approval, "I knew you would smell it! There is no reason to conceal anything from you, my child. So I have to confess that your sense of smell didn't betray you. It's just as good as your father's."

I found this answer to be satisfactory and developed my line of thinking further, "If you confess your guilt, it is all the proof that is needed. I'm all ears."

Zinovi either frowned or smiled, "Klarochka, I don't much appreciate this achievement of legal thought. I'd rather you didn't quote it but relied upon the eternal ancients."

Klara waved her hand at him, "Dad, do you even realize that we could be overheard by somebody? Even walls have ears nowadays. Let's talk about what really matters instead. What's the lucky lady called?"

Zinovi poured some tea for Klara and for himself and kept majestically silent.

"Dear father, isn't it time to end the pause?" Klara said to get him to speak faster. "I hear that even the great actress Vera Komissarzhevskaya didn't pause for such a long time in her monologues."

"Komissarzhevskaya," responded Zinovi in a voice that was as majestic as his silence, "kept silent at work. She did it not because she had no idea what and how to say but, rather, because she wanted to keep her admiring audience in suspense. As for me, sweetheart, I'm very talkative at work, while at home I'm silent. And only because I'm overcome with feelings."

Klara nodded her benevolence and took a sip out of a cup with a light-hearted flower painted on its side.

"I'm glad to hear that this lady, who has until now remained unnamed, provokes a surge of feelings in my father. So?"

"Berta," Zinovi breathed in and out as if preparing to ingest the contents of an entire flask.

"The consistency is very predictable," said Klara in a voice filled with understanding.

They both kept silent for a while as they sipped from their cups.

"Berta Faivelevna," Zinovi clarified. "She is a little younger than I am. . ."

"Come to think of it," Klara observed from her position of superiority, "if Zalmanovna can be transformed into Zinevievna, then let Faivelevna turn into Pavlovna. Let's be consistent, at least. Of course, everything points to the possibility that I will find it more convenient and she will find it more pleasing if we addressed each other with less formality."

Zinovi gave an embarrassed cackle that was not devoid of hidden enjoyment.

"Not to the degree you imply but altogether, you are not mistaken..."

Klara put down her empty cup and concluded to show her complete understanding,

"So finally the situation is becoming clear. Would you like to hear the other side, too, Dad?"

"You are not the other side, sweetheart," Zinovi smiled. "You are the first and foremost, or the most important side in all of this."

"Don't overstate my influence," Klara observed with kindness. "As far as I remember, you managed to accept my choice without too much burning emotion."

"But Samuil never gave me a reason!" Zinovi exclaimed. "What was there to get emotional about?"

"Still, emotions could have become burning. Emotions don't need any special reason to do just that, as you and I should know well enough. I would even say that the punier the reason, the more burning there is, and vice versa."

Klara hugged Zinovi and added, "So here is my opinion, Dad. Don't fear your daughter's jealousy. I will not let you down. Now calm down and tell me more about our Berta."

XLV

The car was rolling down the pavement of Sumskaya Street, leaving behind the Glass Fountain, which was as smooth as a fresh sheet of paper, the indifferently prideful Salamander House, the tiny and exquisite Rymarskaya Street, the noisy and exciting Seminary Hill, the grandiose Blagoveschensky Cathedral with its paintings by Repin, and the Sverdlov Street that was panting because of the unbearable heat. Finally, it reached the Southern railway station.

The Kharkov Railway Square, Klara thought, looked like a miniature Dzerzhinsky Square. Not quite a miniature either, if you look at it objectively. The building of the railway station is very similar to the Gosprom. It might be less huge but, instead, it has high staircases that would look even better if they were covered with a red carpet. The red carpet would lead one majestically to the columns and heavy doors that are as pompous and solemn as the entire Southern railway station.

Samuil and Vladimir Fedorovich carried heavy suitcases while Klara stared at the Railway Square they were leaving behind, the high ceilings of the railways station, the long train platform and, finally, the train that was slowly emerging as if out of a different life-time or an unfinished dream.

"Travel lightly," Vladimir Fedorovich smiled at them, kissed Klara, and shook Samuil's hand. "Send us a post-card when you get there."

"Try not to miss us," Klara said just in case, even as she realized that this was hardly possible.

"Just the opposite!" asked Samuil, enveloping Vladimir Fedorovich in a happy hug. "Miss us and wait for us. We will be back soon, as usual."

The train stewardess removed the stairs people used to get on the train and banged the door shut as if it were an elevator. The train departed from the platform, allowing, in a condescending way, that the people departing and those seeing them off to wave their good-byes and see how Vladimir Fedorovich's straw hat gradually transformed into a small child's cap, a handkerchief, a pin, a distant memory.

XLVI

"Let me guess your last name!" one of the passengers who shared their compartment said in a kind voice that betrayed a Moscow, or even more likely a Leningrad, accent. He was a young man who looked somewhat similar to Samuil, probably because he had similar hair and maybe a similar smile. The other passenger in their compartment was already fast asleep on his upper bunk, without even putting bedclothes on it.

"Your task will be doubly difficult," Klara observed. "We have different last names, until for the moment."

"Exactly!" Samuil confirmed and burst out laughing. "I'm just a simple tin-maker, while Klara. . ."

"A tin-maker?" the passenger exclaimed. "So you and I are namesakes? I mean, we have the same last name?"

"What, you are also Blekhman?" Samuil asked incredulously.

"This is insane!" the other Blekhman clasped his hands in satisfaction. "Let me introduce myself. I'm Alexander Blekhman, a performance artist."

Klara and Samuil were shaken.

"We heard you perform on the radio several times," Klara said and offered him her hand for a handshake. "Klarissa Stolberg."

"There is no need to treat me with such admiration," Blekhman modestly shook Klara's hand and then gave Samuil a firmer handshake. "I will be perfectly content with quite adoration."

"And when were you born?" Samuil inquired.

"Nineteen twenty-two."

"Sania, we are also almost the same age. I was born in twenty-six," Samuil said in a sing-song voice. "Great to meet you. My name is Samuil but I prefer to be called Senia."

"We are both Blekhmans and one of us is Senia while the other one is Sania. Guys, it would be a grievous sin not to drink to this kind of a coincidence," Blekhman exclaimed and started carrying out this plan. "How will the lady feel about this?"

"In a mildly indifferent manner," Klara replied and smiled in a way that almost caused Blekhman to spill the drink that seemed like it would be more than enough to accompany a good train conversation.

"Klara, Senia! I'm drinking to both of you and to all Blekhmans out there!" Blekhman announced. "There are not that many of us in terms of quantity but our quality is outstanding."

The man in the upper bank kept on sleeping like a log. It was hard to understand what was the point of sleeping when one could have a lot more fun being awake.

"So, guys, what is that that you do in life?" Blekhman asked with genuine interest.

"Klara will be a lawyer and I'll become a doctor," Samuil replied in a contented tone. "Sania, why don't you tell us about yourself? You are an excellent performer, believe me. I have an amazing taste, so I should know."

"Yes," Blekhman sighed dreamily, taking a huge bite in order to avoid staring at Klara. "It's a pleasure to talk to people who understand art."

"But not with those who are artificially understanding," Klara laughed and wisely steered the discussion in a more universal direction. "Your environment, I mean the artistic circles, must be very special."

Blekhman smiled and almost imperceptibly shrugged his shoulders, "I have been able to form an opinion on this issue but it is quite subjective."

Klara reassured him, "Sania, it is only the subjective that is of any interest. The objective truths can be found in newspapers."

Both Blekhmans laughed.

"Talking subjectively," Blekhman continued, "my extremely subjective point of view is that while artistic women possess a combination of intellect and emotions, artistic men are pure emotion. A man who is creative is touchy and easy to offend. More than anything in the world he enjoys feeling downtrodden and offended. Artistic men adore throwing creative tantrums, pout in an artful manner, fold their hands on their stomachs, purse their lips, puff their cheeks proudly, and sulk. They sulk whenever they think people haven't given them enough attention and veneration, irrespective of how much attention and veneration is actually offered to them. Sulking is the favorite hobby of creative men. They sulk and pout, pout and sulk, like tiny children who refuse to be potty-trained."

Samuil burst out laughing but still couldn't help voicing an objection, "Sania, I think you are being too rough on them. I'm sure there are all kinds of people among male artists."

"You, for example," Klara condescended to offer a compliment in a manner that was almost as majestic as that of Maria Isaakovna, while trying to avoid laughing out loud. "I can't really imagine you pouting and sulking. I don't think you'd be able to even if you tried."

Blekhman took a sip and agreed, "Of course, there are pleasant exceptions from this rule among men and unpleasant ones among women. Let's say that female artists are also not entirely averse to sulking but they do it out of necessity and not for the sake of enjoyment, like men do."

"Now this is an objective picture," exclaimed Samuil.

Klara added,

"This just goes to show that some subjective opinions can be quite objective.

Blekhman laughed,

"This must be because of my profession. I'm not just any performer. I don't do tragedy or romantic drama, God forbid. As you know, I'm a comedian. My job keeps me on my toes and forces me not to take myself too seriously. As we all know, even those who fear nothing else are afraid of laughter. What choice do I have, then, but to fear my own ridicule at times. This is why I can hardly afford to sulk and pout. The moment I start pouting, I'll see my reflection in a mirror, and will get rid of the pout as soon as I can."

Klara looked out of the window. It was too dark to see anything. Only the lanterns emerged from the darkness from time to time, but they disappeared from view so fast that it was hard to say if they were really there or if one just imagined them.

"I used to have a friend," Klara said. "My mother called her my Sancho Panza. Well, she was Sancho Panza like I was Don Quixote. Nobody could listen to her without smiling, even though she was a very serious person. A very intelligent and serious person. . ."

Blekhman nodded with a contented look, "Hardly anything is more serious humor. Of course, I'm not talking about what I refer to as orange-peel humor."

"Meaning that an orange demands a joke to be made about before being eaten," Samuil asked.

"No, of course not. What I mean is the kind of humor where a person steps on an orange peel, slips and falls down, which is supposed to make the audience laugh out loud. Or the kind of humor where somebody throws a cake into another person's face, which is also supposed to be funny. This genre offers endless creative possibilities."

"You don't like Charlie Chaplin, do you?" Klara asked.

"I don't like the kind of humor that aims for the jugular rather than for the brain," Blekhman explained. "You know what really made me laugh when I was twelve or thirteen years old? When I was reading Dickens's *Hard Times*, I came across the character who was called M'Choakumchild, and I fell off the couch I was laughing so hard. The name itself was so hilarious that it wasn't necessary to imagine the character slipping on an orange peel or getting hit with a cake. Just M'Choakumchild, and that will always be funny."

"One needs to be Dickens in order to come up with something like this," Samuil remarked.

Blekhman developed this idea.

"Of course! But if you can't write like Dickens, you should just go to the dickens instead of trying to pretend you are a genius."

They laughed. Blekhman felt encouraged by their agreement and continued,

"Klara just mentioned Sancho Panza. His name might mean nothing to us, but to a Spaniard, the name "Panza" is both hugely meaningful and funny. In Spanish, "Panza" means "belly.""

"Really?" Samuil laughed in his musical voice. "Or maybe "tummy", as we would call it. That would be even better!"

"I can only imagine," Klara observed, "how appalled Mila would have been had she known what the nickname my mother gave her stood for. Not only was Sancho quite plump, his name was fat, too. Senia, do you remember the kind of figure Mila had? I hope you don't, of course."

"I do. She looked like Queen Victoria on your pre-war stamps. Unfortunately, you can't see anything below the queen's neck but the neck itself is highly expressive."

When everybody finished laughing, Klara continued in a more serious tone,

"Mila was just as beautiful below the neck as she was above it. . . Sania, so how about this story by Chekhov, then, where the clerk sneezed on the general's bald-pate? How is this kind of humor different from the orange peel and the cake in the face?"

"That's exactly what I'm saying!" exclaimed Blekhman. "Chaplin would have just stopped there and let the audience laugh at the sneezing clerk and the general who tries to wipe off the snot. Then, they would start pummeling each other and throwing cakes. Chekhov, however, does something entirely different. The most important part of the story comes after the sneeze. The sneeze is just the beginning, a pretext, a reason to start the story. For Chaplin, though, it would be the culmination."

Samuil both agreed and disagreed,

"You are right, of course, Sania, but the story ends very sadly. The clerk dies, poor creature."

Blekhman nodded in a way that wasn't very sad but that was neither quite happy.

"Guys, I visited so many cities, gave so many performances that I can't even remember all of them anymore. And I have to tell you that people look for humor even where there is none. They try to avoid noticing all the tears that laughter conceals. No matter how funny an author is, if he is talented, he always feels sad deep inside. This is an incomprehensible paradox, a mystery. I hope I will be able to solve it one day. The funnier an author is, a talented author, of course, the sadder he seems if only we read him and think about his work more carefully. The one who never laughs and just tries to scare the readers with all kinds of horrors and nightmares, in reality, never feels sad. He might not be happy but he is definitely not sad. The writer who laughs, only reveals his true feelings to those who want to understand him, that is, the people who are closest to him, such as me and you. This reminds me of a suite by Bach that sounds happy on the surface but is performed in a minor."

Blekhman smiled and added,

"A wise philosopher said that there needs to be no other proof for the existence of God than music. I think he was talking about Bach's music."

Klara looked attentively at both Blekhmans, then glanced out of the window and said in a thoughtful but harsh way,

"For me, the best proof of God's existence would be that those millions of people had not been annihilated. Nobody even knows how many were killed. . ."

The compartment plunged into a silence that was as deep as the one that had been provoked by Samuil's recent announcement that he and Klara were going to the Crimea. There was no more snoring coming from the upper bunk, and even the wheels made almost no noise as they tried to listen and consider what had been said.

"Those millions of people were annihilated, though, which is why, Sania, music does not convince me."

Blekhman sighed and suggested, "Let's drink to the decade of the forties. When I was fighting in the war, it seemed like those years would never come to an end. But now this decade is almost over. And I have no idea whether that's a good thing or a bad thing."

"Probably both, just like it always is," Klara smiled.

"Let's also drink to the fifties," Samuil added. "Let this new decade last for a very long time and let us never decide if we want it to end."

"Exactly," Blekhman nodded. "And let the fifties be free of this one thing I really hate, which is skepticism. I love it when people smile, this is my guiding principle both at work and in life. But I hate it when people smirk."

"We can promise you a lot of smiles," said Klara and smiled again.

"And may nobody even dare smirk!" Samuil agreed.

Food and drink that had looked more plentiful before the conversation started, finally ran out. The two Blekhmans went outside of the compartment to smoke. Samuil gave Klara a touching and pleading look and promised that it would be just this once.

Klara remained sitting at the small table and looking out of the window where the forties were disappearing and gradually melting in the unusual yellowish darkness. She saw the unreal station-house and listened to the announcement made in a loud, clear but incomprehensible voice. You can only get to hear this kind of voice at night at a small station where you will spend a few minutes and then leave forever without anybody even realizing that you were on that train.

Klara kept staring and hoping that the fifties would last for a very long time, and better yet, forever. They hadn't even begun yet, so there would be a very long time before they come to an end...

Klara was staring out of the window, asking herself what Klara was doing at that very moment. Here, Klara's father is getting up, walking outside – here he is, in the hallway – getting some water out of the bucket with a grey mug made out of tin. The water tastes fresh and delicious. He returns back to bed. Here he is, right now, getting into bed and pulling the blanket over himself. And Klara. . . she is staring out of the window, hoping to see the other Klara who right now, this very moment is looking out of the window of her compartment, trying to see her. Klara doesn't want to fall asleep, even though she is very sleepy. And maybe – it really may just be – that she has an inkling of Klara traveling to the Crimea and looking out of the window at this very moment, this very moment in time.

Now, right now, the train slowly started moving again and the announcer's voice remained in the unreal past that has so recently been the present, and the yellow lantern against a black background remained in this very same former present. The train, in the meanwhile, breathed in, breathed out, started moving and continued on its way, towards Simferopol.

There was still such a deliciously long way to go to Simferopol, and Klara looked outside and thought, "Does it really exist, this faraway Crimea?" And she wanted to get there so much that she wished the train would take as long as possible getting there. Endlessly long. . .

As she was falling asleep, she smiled at Blekhman's phrase that reminded her of Hamlet, "Why do I need this person?"

He must have been referring to the man who was snoring mercilessly and severely on the top bunk.

XLVII

Vladimir Fedorovich smiled. He did it both openly and to himself. He smiled as he was walking home from work, riding on a tram from visiting his sister Nadia, talking to the Feldmans in the kitchen, heating up the food Maria had left for him before leaving on her business-trip.

The forties were about to end, but there was still so much life and happiness inside that one could barely avoid smiling. "What else should I do, cry?" would he ask in response to Maria's usual indignant query, "Why do you keep smiling, Petkevich?"

Sometimes, he looked serious, for example when he read a newspaper. However, deep inside, he still kept smiling. When he unwrapped his thousandth lollipop, he also smiled, even though he was sorry he was unwrapping only one lollipop and just for himself. He was still sure, though, or if not sure, then at least hopeful, that this wasn't for long. Samuil and Klara suited each other perfectly. Of course, it would have been a reckless temerity to contradict Maria, which is why he didn't contradict her, thinking that time would tell and everything was going to work out eventually.

Thank goodness, he never ran out of work to do. Every night, Vladimir Fedorovich brought his work back home with him, put on his reading glasses (he didn't need glasses to see far-away objects), wrote without a single cross-out in thick accounting books, snapping his abacus beads with a sound that reminded him of rain-drops hitting a window-sill, or impatient knuckles rapping on a table, or the wheels of a train going to Simferopol...

In the evenings, he would emerge from the gigantic, truly festive entrance to their apartment building onto Sumskaya Street. While Maria was away, he could openly take a cigarette out of his mysterious box made out of an unknown kind of blond wood, light up, and walk down the street with a smile. He would turn onto any of the multitude of streets in Kharkov, all of which let one walk as long as one wanted thinking about how much peace and happiness there was everywhere in sight.

Today, for example, he finished his cigarette, smiled, and entered the building on Mayakovskaya Street where Zinovi Stolberg lived in his communal apartment. In Maria's absence, Zinovi had invited Vladimir Fedorovich to his place in order to introduce him to Berta.

They were sitting together at a round table covered with a light-green tablecloth that matched the color and maybe even somehow the form of the lamp-shade above the table.

"Volodia, Ziama told me that potato pancakes are your favorite dish," Berta placed several pancakes from a deep frying-pan onto everybody's plate. "I hope he wasn't mistaken. But I hear you are not a great fan of sausage, right?"

"Thank you kindly," smiled Vladimir Fedorovich. "Zinovi, with this kind of memory, you will live for a hundred years more. And with a wife like this, a hundred and fifty years on top of that."

"Only if such a drastic change in my personal life doesn't mess up my memory!" laughed out Zinovi. "Of course, there are important aspects of the relationship where the change is not that dramatic. For instance, Berta cooks just as well as Klara."

"How are the kids?" Berta asked.

"I saw them off," Vladimir Fedorovich said with satisfaction. He finished the crunchy crust of the pancake and asked, "So where did you two meet?"

"At work," Berta explained readily. "I saw this lonely man of an age that was not yet hopeless walking down the hallway and trying not to look sad. He doesn't look very happy, I thought. Why don't I make him less lonely and sad?"

Here, Zinovi had to interfere.

"Volodia, look at me. Do you think I look less sad?"

"At this point, I think you definitely do," Vladimir Fedorovich said, laughing. "Berta achieved what she set out to do. I will tell you honestly, they always manage to do whatever they set out to. Take Maria, for example. She wants me not to be too happy, and I'm not too happy. I can't say that I'm sad, either, because Maria would never allow for that to happen. I'm happy, of course, but within limits."

Stolberg and Petkevich clinked their glasses in solidarity, and Zinovi sighed, "You see, Volodia. . . Berta and I have a certain age difference. Klara already knows. I agree that my age is not entirely hopeless, but Berta's age, to the contrary, offers a lot of hope. So this is just a fact. Our age difference is very noticeable."

"Don't exaggerate, Ziama," Berta said and offered a pretty smile. "Or rather, don't diminish."

"It isn't really like your age needs to be either exaggerated or diminished," Vladimir Fedorovich said. "Yours is the best of all ages, and it only will get better with time. I should know. And so should Zinovi."

Petkevich and Stolberg clinked their glasses and exchanged an understanding look. Berta did not object. She nodded in agreement, "Let's say that I'm a woman of Balzac's age, and that's all there is to it."

Vladimir Fedorovich asked with curiosity, "Are you sure you are not exaggerating? In my opinion, you have a long way to go until Balzac's age, Berta."

"I will gladly clarify, Volodia," Berta explained willingly. "It's only women who have this Balzac's age, as we all know, and it is a time period that can be stretched almost indefinitely. I am located right it the beginning of it, just like Eugenie Grandet or Madame Bovary."

"A lady," Zinovi allowed himself to offer a minor correction to Berta's words. "I prefer to call a woman a lady. Madame sounds like a word that should only be used when waiting in line for something."

Berta nodded, poured out the tea into the tea cups decorated with flowers and asked Vladimir Fedorovich, "Volodia, you didn't try the sausage, did you?"

Vladimir Fedorovich smiled in a way that was either critical or mysterious and responded, "I don't eat sausage, may the devil take it."

"There must be some mystery involved," Zinovi exclaimed as he accompanied a sip of his tea with taking a bite of his piece of sausage. "Volodia, please share this story with us!"

"I'd rather it remained a mystery," said Vladimir Fedorovich shaking his head. "Because this is the kind of story that isn't fit to be told or listened to at the table."

Berta looked at Zinovi chew on his piece of sausage with a slightly horrified expression. She let him swallow and said slowly, as a person who was ready for any eventuality, "Ziama, how do you feel?"

Zinovi listened to his body, which seemed to be resting noiselessly.

"Life goes on," said Zinovi uncertainly. "What did you think I was feeling?"

"Life will continue going on," Vladimir Fedorovich laughed. "Just don't think about any silly thing like that. This is why I'm not sharing this story with you. I just avoid sausage as much as I can, that's all."

Berta didn't feel sufficiently reassured. She observed carefully, as if fearful of awakening Zinovi's slumbering body,

"Having too much information is not a good thing. While I never questioned sausage, everything was fine. But now that I discovered this about it, I'll never buy another piece of sausage ever again."

"What did you discover about it, Berta?" asked Vladimir Fedorovich in a guilty voice. "I abstained from telling you anything on purpose."

"If you did share your story," Berta sighed and rested a suspicious glance on a saucer with the remaining few pieces of sausage, "I'd start disliking sausage. Now I'm simply afraid of it."

Zinovi kissed Berta's hand and winked at Vladimir Fedorovich, "I hope there is nothing else of the kind you know."

Of course, Vladimir Fedorovich did know (Petkevich not knowing something?), but he decided not to bother those present with his knowledge, which is why he said, "Those who never visited a meatpacking factory or kagaty (when they heard the word "kagaty", Berta and Zinovi froze, expecting the worst), lacks a lot of crucial knowledge. Fine, since there is no pickled cabbage on this table, I'll tell you. Do you know how cabbage gets pickled?"

Zinovi and Berta gasped as they awaited a horrible revelation.

"Oh, don't get scared," Vladimir Fedorovich laughed. "Kagaty is a place where cabbage is placed in a huge empty swimming-pool. Women jump in there and start stomping on the cabbage in their rubber boots in order to get it to pickle. This is why I never eat it."

Berta unfroze and said, "My mother never stomps on her pickled cabbage."

"And that's great. But at kagaty, it does get stomped at so that it can release juices and start pickling. They stomp on it, and then you get to eat it. If something falls into the swimming-pool, nobody will take the trouble of removing it, and it will be stomped on as part of the pickled cabbage. I remember one of these women looking at me in a severe fashion, as if I was guilty of something, and saying, "To each his own.""

"And who owns people like that?" Zinovi asked.

Vladimir Fedorovich grinned,

"Probably the zoo we have right here around the corner. May the devil take them all. I'd much rather you just told me what your plans are."

While slightly horrified Berta kept silent, Zinovi, who welcomed the change of topic even more than he had the new dish that he'd been served, rattled out, "Volodia, Berta and I have decided to move in together. We will exchange our communal apartments for something more decent."

Vladimir Fedorovich took a sip from his cup and made a practical observation, "What can possibly be more decent than a communal apartment?"

"All communal apartments are different, Volodia," smiled Berta who was starting to recover. "Mine, for example, has all its facilities outdoors."

"I know," Vladimir Fedorovich agreed. "Only these differences don't make much difference. My sister Nadia has the same problem. The facilities are outdoors and all the inconveniences are indoors. She has the same kind of Pipas, Volkovas, and Strelkinas of her own, may the devil take them."

Zinovi nodded, "You are right, Volodia. This is our communal fate. These apartments are noisy and, may the ladies forgive me, lousy. One almost feels like not moving in but just moving as far out as possible. And may the devil take them, as you so rightly observe."

"You will hardly want to move away from me," Berta laughed, kissed Zinovi and continued,

"Outdoor facilities can be seen as a social phenomenon. Have you ever noticed what a person who has to use outdoor facilities dreams about? Let me tell you a scary story. It will be scarier than any meatpacking factory or even kagaty. Fair warning: the story will be terrifying, so if you, my dears, are not completely sure of yourselves, you might be better served going outside right now. There you will be completely safe."

Once she was sure that Zinovi and Vladimir Fedorovich were prepared for everything, Berta began her story.

"In our communal apartment, we have a young family. These are amazing people, a young married couple called Tonia and Fedia. Their last name is Gustokasha. They have a son called Misha who is three and a half years old."

"Klara also wants to call her son Misha," Zinovi observed.

"Maria will never agree to that," Vladimir Fedorovich said, shaking his head.

"I hope Klara's Misha never has to experience what our Misha did!" sighed Berta wistfully.

Zinovi had a tragic premonition, just like the one he'd felt when sausage was discussed.

"Berta," he asked in a half-whisper, "is the kid alive?"

"Bite your tongue, Ziama!" exclaimed Berta. "Would I even be telling the story if the kid, God forbid. . . God help you, Ziama, how could you even think of something like this? Of course, the kid is alive. But just barely, poor mite."

Vladimir Fedorovich smiled, while Berta calmed down a little and continued, "The parents asked Tonia's grandmother, Baba Klava, to stay home with the kid until he is old enough for daycare. The grandmother agreed and moved to Kharkov from her village. She is a good person but she's hard of hearing in both ears. More importantly, she is also tall and as fat as a rhino, especially in the front. And in the back, too, of course."

"Berta," Zinovi murmured, "I never realized you had this tendency to recur to Naturalist descriptions in the style of Emile Zola. It's almost like you've become a completely different person right before my eyes."

"Just hear me out," said Berta and gave an insistent nod that was to serve as a warning to the listeners. "Once, little Misha went to the outdoor facilities to do his business. The outdoor toilet is quite narrow but one can still turn around in there.

And there is a seat. I'm not telling you all this because I love Naturalism but just to make sure you understand the story."

Zinovi and Vladimir Fedorovich looked at each other. Neither of them had the slightest idea about how the seemingly innocent story was going to end. Berta continued, trying to sound as mysterious as possible in order to keep her listeners in suspense.

"Little Misha always found it easy to go into the facility and sit down. He'd come in, take his seat, and stay there as long as he needed. Baba Klava, however, had a lot of trouble trying to get inside the booth. She couldn't squeeze in there sideways because her chest made that impossible. If she just walked in there, she found it impossible to turn around in order to take a seat comfortable. The only remaining option was for her to remove her underwear before entering the toilet, bend over, and enter the facility by walking backwards. She always introduced herself into the little booth very slowly and carefully to avoid catching her shoulder on the wall or hitting her head against the toilet's ceiling."

Vladimir Fedorovich and Zinovi seemed to start realizing what was going to happen. They were afraid, however, to confess what it was that they had started to realize. Berta, in the meanwhile, continued her story with an implacable determination to get it to the ending that could have become tragic.

"Tonia and Fedia don't allow little Misha to lock the toilet door from the inside. They want to make sure that in case something happens to the kid, they will be able to rush in and save him, without wasting time on breaking the door down. So little Misha went into the toilet and had barely had time to sit down, when suddenly the door opened, and he saw a hugely grandiose backside of Baba Klava moving towards him."

As they imagined this scene, the men felt their blood run cold, inhaled and forgot to exhale. Berta didn't allow them to recover their senses and continued her story.

"If you, two grown men, are so terrified, just imagine what the poor child must have felt! Little Misha screamed, yelled, cried, but Baba Klava's backside – I call it that to avoid making this description too naturalistic – kept moving in his direction. She didn't hear his screams because, as I said, she **is** hard of hearing."

"How hard of hearing do you have to be not to hear a scared child scream?" Zinovi finally managed to exhale.

"Between the child and Baba Klava's ears, Ziama, her humongous backside was located, that same backside that was moving towards the child like the "Tiger" tank."

"Do you remember, Berta, how I told you what we used to do to those tanks during the war?" Zinovi commented.

"I can imagine," Vladimir Fedorovich smiled. "Did the kid chase Baba Klava all the way to Berlin, like you guys did with the German tanks?"

Berta triumphantly finished her story.

"He chased her even further than that. When Baba Klava's huge behind came close to little Misha's face, he bit it with all his might. He practically took a chunk out of it with his teeth so that poor Baba Klava grabbed her, to use a polite term, underwear and ran out of the scary facility. She was yelling so loud that she even managed to hear her own screams. She told us that herself when we went to see her at the hospital."

"And what about the kid?" asked Vladimir Fedorovich and Zinovi who still didn't dare to laugh.

"Dr. Gilman cured him," Berta reassured the men. "He prescribed showers, relaxing conversations, and a nutritious diet. Of course, Tonia had to take care of the child's diet while Baba Klava was hospitalized."

At this point, the men finally allowed themselves to burst out laughing. Their laughter was so loud that the neighbors were forced first to cough several times, then to cough louder, and eventually to knock on the wall, the ceiling, and most unexpected of all, the floor. Of course, it wasn't all that unexpected. While Zinovi laughed, he stomped his feet so much that even Baba Klava could have heard him.

When he came outside, Vladimir Fedorovich took a cigarette out of his mysterious box and slowly went home, to Sumskaya Street. As he walked, he kept thinking that Klara's high school friend Mila could come to look a little like Berta once she reached the age of one of Balzac's female characters. As for Klara, she was more beautiful now and would probably remain so in the future.

He also thought that being forty-five years old might not be considered Balzac's age, especially since men don't have such an age, but still, it was a good, tranquil and cozy age, at least as long as everybody was in good health.

He considered this idea, took a drag of his cigarette, and silently added, "And as long as there is no war."

XLVIII

In the Crimea – oh, my God, was that even possible, the Crimea? – you suddenly find yourself in a completely different kind of life.

The train stops in Djankoi for the prescribed twenty minutes, and you feel something that back in Kharkov never happened to you and, in all probability, could not have happened. You wake up early. Everybody else is still asleep, and you are not even sure that all of this is really happening to you at this very moment. You lift yourself up on your pillow and look out of the window. The train platform is mysterious, strange, but strange in a pleasing, welcoming way. It's so early, and the stillness of the compartment is Kharkov-like, carried over from far away.

On the train platform, there is a different dimension to all that can be measured. That is where the Crimea starts. Women with buckets that are covered with lids, and there is probably something deliciously crunchy underneath those lids. . . The station-master. . . The porters. . . All of these people awakened a long time ago and are now busily going about their day. They all know where and why they are hurrying, and it is as if in this Crimean world people never slept. Of course, they must go to sleep some time but I cannot even begin to imagine them sleepy or actually asleep. . .

I will inhale the early morning air now. It smells of Djankoi, which means that it smells of the Crimea. Already this is the Crimea. . . The Crimea that has appeared in front of me in a way that was both expected and sudden. I knew it existed, it had to exist, but still, I thought,

"My God, does it really exist? I know it does, but is it even possible that it should be real?" I never confessed my fairy-tale doubts to anybody, however.

And now here it is, the Crimea. It isn't something I invented. Could I ever hope to invent anything like it?

But if it isn't an invention, then where did the Crimea come from? It wasn't there, even though I knew it existed, and now, all of a sudden, it's right here. It's one thing to know that the Crimea exists and even to know everything there is to know about it. It's an entirely different thing, though, to wake up and before I have even been able to become completely awake to see it: here it is, the Crimea.

I have arrived here in a train compartment that after a night that is now almost over and a morning that has suddenly arrived has become as quiet as one of Professor Fuks's lectures. I have arrived on a train with curtained windows in its endlessly empty and long hallway behind the doors that were closed for the night. On a train whose humongous wheels are tapped by the lineman's light hammer. This reminds me of a dentist – I have no idea how I even arrived at such a comparison, this is too funny – tapping the teeth of his patient who is trying hard not to burst out laughing. "Stolberg, your teeth are perfectly healthy."

Or, "Stolbehg," as Rose-Fingered Maiden would have pronounced my last name.

Djankoi smells of sandstone and sea-shells. This entire Crimea has this aroma. For me, Kharkov does, too, even though they are so different from each other, and it's great that they are. The mysterious morning-time crunchy goods in the huge olive-colored buckets covered with lids, this train, the compartment windows that offer me a glimpse of a pale-pink train-station bring together these different parts of the world: Kharkov (God, does it even exist somewhere in the past?) and the Crimea that I both did and didn't expect, and kept preparing myself for... The Crimea that turned out to be so sudden, the Crimea that emerged in front of me also belongs to me.

The train accompanied its own journey with the music it created by clanging against the rails. It hurried by smaller stations where strict station-masters stood with their little raised flags and disappeared before one could see them clearly. It passed by the trees with their narrow silvery green leaves, by the yellowish houses, and by the stretches of land that probably concealed – did they really and truly? – the sea...

A long way before Simferopol, the Crimean sun, which was so different from the Kharkov sun, woke up everybody in their compartment. Blekhman started to sing, rolling his Rs in the same way as Charles Perrot must have rolled them when he told his "Little Red Riding Hood" or "Cinderella" fairy-tales to the adoringly grateful audience,

"In Singapore,
The land of lemon and banana trees..."

"I also love the songs by Vertinsky," Klara smiled, as she struggled not to miss the moment when the sea would emerge at the horizon.

Samuil kissed her and objected,

"He is a little too saccharine for my taste. I don't mean Blekhman, of course. I'm talking about Vertinsky."

"No, Senia, you are wrong," Blekhman laughed. "He sings of lemons, which means his songs can't be all that sweet. A reasonable touch of acidity always helps."

This wasn't the first time that the train traveled down this road that looked like a ladder placed between Kharkov and Simferopol. The train seemed to hurry, but at the same time it also cunningly prolonged the pleasure. The sea continued its tantalizing refusal to emerge.

"I'm going to consider what a touch of acidity needs to do to be recognized as reasonable," Klara responded to Blekhman gaily, kissed Samuil and went into the corridor that had already stopped being empty and endless.

She stood in front of the window, with her head half-tuned towards it. The wind was laughing and tousling her black hair and the white curtains with the beautiful Shevchenko monument painted on them. The wheels clacked in a peaceful and dreamy way. They rapped like impatient fingers on a table, like the abacus beads, like rain drops against a window-sill. The wind made Klara squint but she kept staring at the dry salty earth the train was passing by and at the silvery greenish trees that didn't have a single lemon or banana tree among them. And where would these lemon and banana trees come from if she couldn't even imagine what they looked like.

Suddenly, she exploded with laughter and said (to herself, of course, since Mila wasn't there to say this to Klara),

"What's wrong with you, Stolberg? You sound like that stupid Rosenblum person and not like somebody who got a gold medal upon graduation. If you are in the Crimea, you need to see the sea immediately. You just have to have it in front of you. God, where would the sea even come from around here? This land is completely dry. It's drier than the Sahara desert. And it's covered in salt that crunches on the teeth like salted fish. Maybe a long time ago there was a dinky little sea in these parts. Since then, however, it has all dried up. Not even a dab of iodine remains, just salt."

Mila and Klara would laugh, and all the passengers would feel tranquil and happy because these two beautiful dark-haired girls who had grown so much since their times on Chernyshevskaya Street were so happy and tranquil.

In the meanwhile, the sea is still so happily far away from here and one can go on dreaming about it. First you need to get to Simferopol, then get into a fairytale bus that rolls smoothly across the joyful hills of the Crimea without stopping for three whole hours, and you keep dreaming for the sea to finally appear in front of you. But at the same time you keep wishing for it to torture you for a little bit longer and not to emerge for a while...

The train clanged, puffed and stopped. It waited patiently for the passengers to leave it in peace. The stewardess opened the door, lifted the steps, and it felt like they were looking out of their elevator back in Kharkov. Finally, the train had arrived in this city whose name sounded like a fresh white marshmallow, Simferopol.

The two Blekhmans hugged each other. Blekhman kissed Klara's hand and hurried towards the huge group of people awaiting him at the station.

Klara and Samuil laughed in anticipation of the endless Crimea road and the blue or maybe aquamarine sea that was hiding somewhere beyond the green hills. Then, they started walking towards the bus station.

XLIX

"Good afternoon, Mary Isaakovna," said Pipa almost bending over in self-abasement. She seemed terrified to have been glimpsed by Maria but happy that all she got was a single glance.

Maria nodded dispassionately and went into her room. Her business trip was over. Volodia had come to meet her at the train station, took her home, and went back to work. She still had a couple of hours to put herself together and then, as usual, as thank God endlessly and always, to go down Sumskaya Street, then cross Dzerzhinsky Square, and enter the Engineering House. It is still golden but it doesn't soar anymore because it looks weighed down after the construction work that was done on it. The good news is that Strelkova's time is over. Not in the general sense of the word, smiled Maria, but in the strictly utilitarian sense.

In any case, what did she care about Strelkova? She hadn't been able to sleep on the airplane or on the train. Even when she was talking about work that she was so good at, she kept talking to Klara in her mind. Her daughter was saying something back, but what was there for her to say in response to such convincing arguments?

Maria kept finding new arguments that sounded even more impressive and convincing. Klara still objected, simply because of her innate contrariness. Maria still tried to convince her, silently, calmly, with self-assurance, without losing control, as if she were swimming across the Dnieper with slow, unstoppable strokes.

The more persuasive she was, the farther she found herself from her daughter, as far as the shore of the Dnieper where Rechitsa was located was from the opposite shore. There was no going back anymore, but reaching the other shore wasn't yet possible. Or was it not possible anymore?

The bust on the cupboard shelf stared past her as if trying to say,

"I'm not going to help you out. You will deal with this perfectly on your own. You have faced much greater hardship in your life. And if you start asking for help, you'll only have yourself to blame."

Mary tried to deal with it but that didn't seem possible. And if it wasn't possible for her, then nobody else could have dealt with it.

Petkevich isn't to be relied upon. He seems content with everything. I wish I had his kind of tranquility which seems completely baseless. He is calm and happy but tried not to show it out of solidarity. But all that solidarity of his is fake.

In reality, she has no idea what it is that makes him so happy. If it weren't for her authoritative stare, he'd go off the deep end completely. And he is a respectable person. That's some respectability, may the devil take it, as he'd say.

The water kept dripping from a leaky faucet, as if it had an attack of tachycardia. I'll have to get somebody in to repair it. Nobody's replaced these faucets for years, and this dripping will one day give me a heart attack.

Maria dusted two watches with lids and chains that lay on a bookshelf. The grey watch was smaller, and it had been given to Vladimir Fedorovich Petkevich for his birthday. The white watch was bigger and it had been inscribed to Maria Isaakovna Krupetskaya. Their birthdays were close to each other. Petkevich's was on September 2, and hers on September 5. This must have been why her watch was bigger. Maria smiled and pulled out a drawer. Klara's medal was a shiny pure gold, the book was open on her favorite place. There were two more medals in the drawer, Petkevich's and hers, for valiant labor.

On the bookshelf, there was a fairly old book with mother-of-pearl covers that stood squeezed among other books. Maria had given it to Klara a long time ago, before the war, when they'd still been living in Pushkin Entry. There was a line in this book about how no happiness exists. Maria had no idea that Klara had started to realize that it did exist.

Maria also knew, of course, that happiness existed because she was still so young. Every morning, she would walk down the Sumskaya Street towards Dzerzhinsky Square. On Sumskaya Street, there were the world's best monument to the poet Shevchenko, and the Glass Fountain that resembled her new chiffon scarf and a tiny Gosprom.

Her heels clicked against the pavement as she walked, as usual, without getting into a rush, to design yet another power station. Nobody in the entire country could do it better than she did. The Sumskaya Street floated slowly past the Salamander House, the huge bank, the Pushkin Square, and the festive Ukrainian theater. Then it led to the Tevelev Square where buildings designed before the Revolution by the famous Professor Beketov smiled at Maria with their crystal-clear windows. Lower down, she could see a tranquil grey building constructed a long time ago, in 1925.

After work, she would sometimes come out on the balcony alone to stare into the skies that had blessed her with the miracle of her happy life.

She was still very young. There were still two entire months to go before she would turn forty.

L

The bus was placidly climbing a huge, overhanging Crimean mountain. Its wheels were drawing complex flourishes on the smooth highway made of dry asphalt. They felt as if a strong soft palm of Pushkin's giant had playfully but carefully lifted them above the ravines, the hillsides that were hurrying downwards, the sea that had still not dared to show itself, and the entire rapidly diminishing world. They had no idea what was making their heads swim. Was the high altitude, love that was clutching at their throats, or the sun that was as red in its morning glory as nutmeg?

There were no words to describe everything they were feeling. Even if such words existed, what could they have managed to or dared to narrate? How could they, in the absence of smell or color, transmit the singing aquamarine placidity and the overwhelming correctness of the sweet and sour vineyards, the mysterious hieroglyphics of the Crimea road, and, most importantly, the expectation of seeing the sea that was soaring above the ravines like an unseen, invisible sea-gull?

And then, all of a sudden, like a burst of thunder in the midst of a clear blue sky, it appeared. It was as if the entire world suddenly clapped its soundless and loud-sounding hands. The mountains roared with laughter, the wrinkles of the pathways on the ancient hillsides uncurled, and the vineyards joyfully pointed with their elongated grapes,

"Here it is, here it is, finally. The sea! It's right there, beneath you, there it goes!"

Suddenly, without warning, unexpectedly, all of a sudden. The sea, the epitome of all things unexpected that nobody managed to understand completely. Completely? Not even a tiny little bit. The sea! Can anybody really expect it? Can the sea be expected? You can wait for it as long as you want but it will still catch you unawares. It is like a mysterious surprise, like one of the gifts for one of your very first birthdays that your mother placed on the chair next to your bed during the night. When you wake up in the morning, you know that the gift must be lying next to you, and all you have to do is open your eyes. And then you open your eyes and can't believe what you are seeing because the gift is so amazing, so incredible, and so fantastic.

The sea jumped out at them. It appeared between the mountains and the horizon like a wink from an exotic beauty whose green eye flashed for a moment and then concealed itself behind the eye-lid of the mountains. You emit a disappointed sigh. The sea has finally shown itself but there is still a long way to go, an entire endless hour. Right when you think this, though, the sea prevents you from going on sighing and jumps out at you like a cork from a champagne bottle, and you will not be able to tear yourself from it ever again.

Here it is, the Crimea that can be neither painted nor described with words. The multicolored names of its cities nobody could have invented. You can only hear them at Eastern bazaars or in the majestic Ancient Greece. These colorful names are sweet like halva: a purple city, a yellow one, a magenta one, two red twins, the snow-white city...

You will inhale the Crimea, drink it with your eyes, ears, your entire body, like the statue of a bear at the foot of the golden city. It is so solid, so free of all cares and cages, unlike the bear in the Kharkov zoo. It's a real bear, which is more than an owner of the city. He is a true tsar who abandoned his royal lair to stand here and lap up the salty and refreshing sea-water in his solid and lazy manner.

You will also cover your mouth with your palm and will stare in awe at the castle that looks like a crown of the queen of swallows. The castle seems to float up in the purple skies next to the city whose bright red name reminds one of the gentle splashing of water under a ship's prow. Above all this aquamarine and violet water, sea-gulls soar. They look like the snow-white butterflies from Pushkin Entry that have grown older.

Close by, in a city whose name is as ancient as Greece itself, you will not be able to stop staring at the castle that looks whiter than the whitest white. You will feel as if the bust you left behind for a short while in your book case has come alive and is smiling at you. It will smile and look at you attentively as you will be climbing the stairs in one of the purple cities towards the Count's castle that is more luxurious than the castles of many a tsar. In the meanwhile, you will be wondering how all these marble lions that are so proud of their African origins managed to find their way here. Downstairs, a purple boat will be rocking softly in the waves.

The waves will chatter about something unknown in a city called after a mysterious, incredible kind of fish. This is a city that has climbed a rocky mountain with its ancient but still quite solid Genovese fortress. The mountain is sleepily counting the innumerable sheep made of sea-foam that keep appearing and disappearing beneath its feet.

The train carefully enters the city with an unheard-of violet-colored name. This name sounds as if somebody had called after a beautiful Schismatic and the echo of her name remained forever hanging over the small houses that are rushing obediently towards the mountains. And this magical city that has now turned out to be real is where the train pulls in very carefully. It is in no rush to pass by the embankment, the sandy beach, and the monument to the greatest of experts in the colors and shades of the sea. Behind his back and right in front of his eyes, his and our multi-colored sea lies in his paintings.

And right over there, at an impossible and safe distance, there is a sea of dead swells that threatens to mesmerize you and rock you to sleep. You won't feel afraid of it, though, because you are sure that **he**, just like the sailor in Rechitsa, will protect you, keep you safe, wake you up in time.

In the evening, the sun will slip into the water like a piece of carrot does when it is dropped into a pot of stock. Kharkov's Glass Fountain will pretend that it has transformed into the Black Sea. In the almost soundless water, a colorful sea will light up with the lanterns of the gently rustling embankment and the port that is quiet at this late hour. The moon will play its eternal sonata and then slowly and a little condescendingly will move towards the horizon. From there, it will spill a generous handful of silvery salt into the sea. The salt will shine like the old silver rubles. I had no hope of finding them anywhere, but now I can see that they are right here, having been spilled by mistake into the Black Sea.

"When I look at the sky, Klara, it makes me wonder," Samuil will sigh and speak Ukrainian and Russian at the same time. "The world has turned out to be so immense. In comparison, we are so tiny, just like diminutive specks in somebody's eye. This makes me sad."

And I will reply immediately because I will be thinking the same thing,

"But we have an immense world right inside ourselves. And that world is much bigger than the one outside."

When the night ends, you will ask yourself whether he is singing his best song ever and his voice breaks because of love and anxiety, or maybe this is the broken falsetto of the salty sea wind that is driving us crazy. And you will ask yourself whether her hair smells of the early morning sea, or maybe the waves flow about like her hair and smell of it.

And then you will both burst out laughing at the sea-gull that is soaring above the purplish green water looking as proud as an albatross. The sea-gull is of the same color as a faded pillow-case, and it will remind you of either an Arkul crow or a regular sea duck. Most of all, of course, it looks like a wet chicken, only its stare is hilariously undomesticated and haughty in the bird's awareness of its ugliness.

You will also laugh - Sic transit gloria mundi! - at the stone that falls as flat as a bad joke into the water and jumps across the waves like a purposeful frog. It won't be able to stay jumping for long. Soon its smooth nose will plunge into the water and only a memory will remain of a stone that looked so self-important as it was laying on the beach but then exhausted itself by jumping and sank in the sea.

You will laugh when a shirt gets torn on a pointy roof of a tiny house on the way to the beach. You will laugh and discuss how in Voroshilovgrad one first needed to climb onto the roof of a house to tear a shirt on it. In the Crimea, though, it is entirely possible to be walking quietly and inoffensively and still get a roof to scratch you like an angry cat, which makes you feel as if you had grown taller than buildings. Because that's just how the Crimea is.

And most importantly, you will laugh because your life is just beginning and it is so endless. The mountains and the horizon protect it from ever coming to an end. And where is that non-existent end? Is it behind the mountains or behind the horizon? And will it ever come anyways?

I never want to forget all this. If I never forget, it will never end, so I will always have it. Right now, at this very moment, I'm standing here and looking at the sea, and I absolutely have to remember this moment forever. The past is no different from the future and the present. It is, in fact, both the future and the present. If you forget nothing, then the past will never become past. It will remain in the present and stretch into the future. And right now, at this very moment, Klara is staring and thinking about me as I think about her, and this is something I also should avoid forgetting. Then, Klara will always stay there in the same, albeit also in a completely different way, and she will also think and remain alive as long as I do.

The sea keeps clutching at the shore just like love is clutching at the throat.

And everywhere, both inside and out, there will be peace and freedom, freedom and peace because happiness consists of freedom and peace, even though the book with the mother-of-pearl covers that I received as a gift said that no happiness exists. It took me twelve years to realize that it does.

Maybe that's why the poet said what he did? To make people think, disagree, and realize?

LI

Fira Markovna was tasting Daniil Savvich's favorite borscht and adding salt to it. She sang in a very impressive way,

"I know that every ship at sea
Always comes to anchor,
But that is something we can't do,
We, homeless wandering artists."

"How did you even manage to get tickets to the concert? I really envy you," she said without a single sign of envy, and sang on a higher note,

"In Singapore,
The land of lemon and banana trees..."

"Senia can do anything he proposes to," Klara said with pride but without condescension, and stirred her own borscht.

"You don't seem to be in any hurry to get there," Fira Markovna said. "I can only imagine how many people will be there. Folks are ready to spend hours waiting just to see a celebrity. And then those who really need to attend the concert don't get a chance."

Klara sighed.

"I'm so sorry, Fira Markovna, but he only managed to get two tickets. Please don't be upset. Maybe even Senia can't do absolutely everything he proposes to."

Fira Markovna waved her hand at Klara and sang, accentuating the "r",

"Your lover was from Portugal,
Or maybe a Malaysian, too..."

"Az och und vey, Klara! Let this be our biggest trouble. You better tell me, sweetheart, when you want me to start sewing your wedding dress. This is not a task to be hurried through, so tell me well in advance, will you?"

Klara smiled and nodded gratefully.

Samuil has been proposing to Klara for years. At first, she simply didn't object, then she accepted. That acceptance, however, remained nebulous and did not acquire the tangible forms Samuil would have wished for.

"It seems," she observed as they were approaching the Law School and Samuil was once again starting to feel like a cat on a hot tin roof, "it seems like you, Dr. Blekhman, are desperate to get married. Am I right?"

"Of course!" Samuil reacted as fast to the word "married" as that same cat would to the word "milk." "Aren't you desperate too, Klarochka?"

Klara paused for a seemingly intolerable length of time, and Samuil inquired in an anxious voice, "Why did you suddenly become so quiet at such a crucial moment in time?"

Klara gave him an encouraging kiss.

"Doctor, you need to hasten slowly or maybe slow down your haste, whichever you prefer. You and I, however, don't need to be in any hurry since nobody is chasing after us. Why get married when we still have two more years of college ahead of us and there is no hint of either a job or a place to live for either of us?"

She paused again and added by way of farewell,

"Go study, I'll check whether you did later."

Having said that, Klara approached the beautiful building of her Law School where she still had two more years to study and where she was at the top of her class. To all effects and purposes, she was already a lawyer. Samuil, in the meanwhile, gave a broad wave of his hand that looked like he was trying to broaden the street with it and went back to his place. He still hadn't received a concrete answer to his question, so there was no news Klara could communicate to Fira Markovna.

While Klara was pouring out the borscht to Maria Isaakovna, Vladimir Fedorovich and, finally, to herself, Maria dared to broach the most important question,

"Klara, my dear, tell your mother the truth. What do you see in this guy? You and he are so different. . ."

"Mother," said Klara patiently but without sadness, "I always tell you the truth, and I will do the same now. Mother, things would be much worse if Samuil and I were the same."

She kissed Maria and added,

"I'm pretty happy with myself. And to be honest, since I like the original so much, I would only feel annoyed by a copy. Besides, he and I are supposed to be different. That's what makes our relationship both possible and convenient. I'm sure you know what I mean."

Maria looked away and tried to change the topic, "How is he doing at school?"

Then she added in a strict tone,

"Petkevich, why do you keep smiling? What kind of a person are you? You just sit there smiling on purpose to annoy me."

Vladimir Fedorovich murmured,

"What should I do then, cry? If I started crying, you'd immediately ask, "Petkevich, why are you crying on purpose to annoy me?""

"How is borscht?" Klara said to put an end to the argument. "Have you noticed how talented I am?"

Vladimir Fedorovich was eating the borscht with an appetite that provided her with an answer to this question. Maria also didn't look too annoyed and even said,

"Good job, sweetheart."

When she saw the pacifying effect her creation had on Maria Isaakovna, Klara found it appropriate to explain,

"Senia was born to be a doctor. He must have been a doctor even before he was born."

"And I thought he was born to be a singer," Maria said, simmering down but resisting it.

"There isn't much difference," Klara shrugged her shoulders. "It all depends on what your disease is. Some people use bel canto to get better. Give me a moment; I need to go fetch the potatoes."

"Thank you so very much," Vladimir Fedorovich said...

...In the evening, she went to get dressed thinking that she needed to hurry because Samuil must be on his way.

LII

Samuil was close by. He was coming from Dobrokhotova Street by a tram.

In order to get his parents to realize that he deserved a chance to live in conditions that, as Klara said, remotely resembled the normal ones, Samuil had spent two semesters sleeping on the desk at school and washing up in the icy water of the Med School's bathrooms.

Finally, just as Mikhail Petrovich had predicted, one of the mamma's boys and papa's girls had failed enough exams to make them eligible for expulsion, and Samuil was accepted as a full-time student in their place. Semen Mikhailovich and Rosa Samoilovna decided that now their son was a respectable man, a future doctor, and allowed him to live at their place on Dobrokhotova Street.

He lived with his parents, his elder sister Ida and her daughter Maia. He took a tram to school, and it only took him about an hour to get there. Dobrokhotova was a tiny, quiet street. One could say that it was pretty miserable, but Samuil learned to like it. He got used to living there almost at once. There was a lot of dust, and the train-station was close by, but living there was not the same as simply coming by for a visit. Who cares that the facilities are outside? At least you can close the door behind you, unlike the bathroom at his vocational school. And you can wash up at the outside sink, or go to the public baths, so what's the problem?

The tram was great, too, because it took him right to the city center and almost to Klara's building. You get out on the corner of Dzerzhinsky and Basseinaya, cross the street, run past the grocery store, and find yourself right at the doors of Klara's place. And while you are on the tram, you can breathe in Kharkov's tram air and think about everything in the world, mostly about Klara, of course, but about many other things as well.

For instance, Samuil thought about how much he disliked the phrase "Do no harm."

"What's the point of having a doctor who is capable of nothing more than not doing harm?" Samuil exclaimed in his thoughts. "You just stand next to the poor patient's bed, hold his hand, click your tongue, and go home to eat your kneidlach soup. Such a doctor has done no harm, so what? Is that why one breaks one's back working for six years, passes horrible, useless exams, learns not to lose consciousness in the anatomical theatre, smile, prod, inject, auscultate? And all that just to do no harm?!"

He emitted such a loud sarcastic click of his tongue that the passengers of the tram glared at him in indignation. Why was such a respectable young man clicking his tongue like a regular syavka? Samuil, however, cared nothing about the passengers. Or he did, of course, he did, how could he even think something like this? But the passengers were healthy, so let them just go on their way and stop interfering with his thoughts.

Samuil agreed with Professor Katsnelson.

"The absence of evil does not, in itself, constitute good," Katsnelson used to say. "The absence of good, however, does constitute evil."

"A doctor should do good, and not just avoid doing harm," Samuil was relieved at having formulated this idea and almost burst out into his favorite song. The passengers, however, were so solemn in its rejection of extraneous emotions that Samuil simply announced out loud,

"My dear friends! The best of health to you!"

And he jumped out into the street to take a walk and to think about what really mattered, namely, Klara.

The passengers were now quite content. It could have never even occurred to them that just three or four years ago they considered this young man who might not be all that self-important and imposing (Samuil, that self-important and imposing?) but who was still quite decent-looking to be a syavka. They could have never guessed it was the same young man who had smiled at them in this annoying way and wished them the best of health. Maybe it was because Klara had been feeding me and I didn't look like a starveling to their eyes? I wasn't so thin I could hide behind a tree branch any longer, even though I still weighed a lot less than the norm. Well, who cares about all these norms anyways?

Or maybe it happened because it seemed unlikely that he would emit a loud Arkul whistle or regale them with either a regular whistle, or a wolf whistle, or even a pucker whistle. Of course, he was actually likely to do it (for Samuil to be unlikely to do it?), but he simply abstained from doing it, which pacified the passers-by. Their tranquility made him feel incredibly calm and joyous, and he felt like whistling so badly that he kept wondering how he managed to stop himself from doing it, and admiring Klara for being so good for him. He still had three more years to go before graduation, but he was one of the best students already. In reality, he had already become a doctor.

LIII

"How many flour sacks did he have to lug to get this kind of biceps?" Klara smiled to herself and to Samuil. She was holding his arm, and they were walking down an alley in the Shevchenko Gardens. They walked in silence, thinking about what Klara called the exact opposite, namely, each other. They stared at people, the benches, the lacquered chestnuts that had dropped from the trees and that looked as if they had been washed in the Glass Fountain before being placed in prickly green containers.

The sun was winking with the last of that day's rays and floating back home to set down behind the old, broken Klochkovskaya Street and the grandiose cathedral. Tomorrow, the sun was going to emerge on the other side in the childish game of hide-and-seek, laughing at its own notorious cunning.

"Huckle Buckle Beanstalk," Klara remembered the unforgettable game she used to play as a kid. This was where she and Vladimir Fedorovich had encountered the condescending German shepherd and the fearless little mouse. This was the exact place where a wet spot had been left as a reminder of undaunted mettle. The zoo was right down that alley. Klara never went there again because she didn't feel like seeing the hassled bears who had been stripped of their forest glory, the tigers and lions who had forgotten their savannah grace, let alone the seven elephants who were grey with their routine ordinariness and who only remotely resembled her sleek cupboard elephants with their sense of security in themselves and their owner.

A little to the left, next to the staircase that led from the Shevchenko Gardens to the dusty and torturous cage-like Klochkovskaya Street, there was a summer theater, and that was where Klara and Samuil were walking, together with all those people they were not noticing. The theater was ordinary and that was what made it beautiful. There was a baby grand piano on the stage, and the lights were bright, even though they were still unnecessary. The people were taking their seats and looking around. A theater is the only place where people stare this way, noticing things and whispering their observations in secret into each other's ears.

The light kept getting more and more necessary, and finally the whispers, the observations and the comments dried up because a pianist approached the baby grand piano. A tall middle-aged man slowly walked to the piano. He was well familiar to everybody, but at the same time he was just as mysteriously unknowable. He carried himself in a way that would have made a member of the royal family from Klara's favorite eighteenth century feel envious. Samuil and Klara exchanged a look, smiled mysteriously and lost themselves in the familiar unreal romance. It sounded like an intangible gift for their upcoming big event that had been composed by this incredible man who had come to visit them either from the salon of a character in Leo Tolstoy's novel, from a Loire castle, or maybe from a palace on the Gulf of Finland.

He was playfully rolling his "r"s in a way that would have found Rose-Fingered Maiden's complete approval. He would raise his voice like a glass of Veuve Clicquot champagne, hold his precious high note like an experienced waiter who holds a tray full of drinks over the heads of his customers, and having tortured his audience with an endlessly short wait, he would lower it, securely and rapidly, without having spilled a drop, and hand the contents of the glass over to Klara and Samuil.

He sang, opening himself up to them, but even after that he remained aristocratically inaccessible and closed.

They couldn't remain sitting. Without moving from their seats or making themselves noticed (as if anybody could have noticed them), they walked around the Shevchenko Gardens and stood for a moment next to the fountain that was floating down the artificial ledges towards the clean, graceful and shiny Klochkovskaya Street. The water was forming a bay that was wide and deep enough to house boats and schooners and even decent ships. They were not only decent-sized and decent-shaped but also manned by crews that looked very decent. There wasn't a single sailor who could have been a lover of rum or who was one-eyed and had a wooden leg. Klara and Samuil both laughed out loud when they saw that.

They stepped down the slabs that led to Klochkovskaya Street. It was decorated with shimmering Chinese lanterns and smelled of playful lemon trees that glowed in the colorful lighting.

"Finally," Maria Isaakovna said. "I was sure you were going to be late as usual."

She kissed Klara and shook Samuil's hand.

"The boarding has been announced," Vladimir Fedorovich said helping Klara climb the gangway that was shaking like an old bridge in Rechitsa. "The forecast promised showers. Call us from time to time."

"Can you ever stop asking them of trivial things, Petkevich?" Maria Isaakovna said in a strict voice, just to hide away her tears.

"Good-bye, Klara, good-bye, Senia!" Berta waved at them and offered Zinovi a good-willed hint, as she took his hand, "I wouldn't object to taking this kind of a honeymoon trip either."

"I'll see what I can do," Zinovi responded. "The good news is that this, at least, depends on nothing but ourselves."

"Sweetheart, drop us a couple of lines whenever you can," Zinovi kissed Klara and hugged Samuil.

An efficient Malaysian sailor removed the gangway and cast off. A concerto by Sarasate was playing slowly and majestically, announcing the departure of their ship. The coastal Klochkovskaya Street lined with greenish and red orange trees that looked like squirrels sitting on the fir-trees and lit with lemony lanterns let their ship set out on their wedding journey. They might have been going to Singapore. Or maybe to Hong Kong, or even Macao. They had no idea where they were going. And who can possibly know such things for sure?

LIV

The beet borscht that Rosa was so proud of and that the entire family adored was very good. Still, today it didn't manage to make anybody happy. To the contrary, for the very first time, it made people feel annoyed. Semen Mikhailovich and Rosa Samoilovna were sitting at the table without exchanging a single look or casting a glance towards the pan that was covered with a lid. Maia was still at school. Ida was at work. They were bound to come home any moment.

And Samuil was going to bring her for a visit any day now. That was going to happen very soon.

The days of hunger they had had to experience were now over. Samuil could now come back and live at their place. He became a respectable person, studied to become a doctor, and brought a student stipend home. He was on fire, metaphorically, of course, not literally. He always brought them gifts, especially for the International Women's Day and everybody's birthdays. He'd kiss his mother, hug his sister, pat his niece on her head, and ask his father about how things were going at the factory.

And then, all of a sudden, he just comes out and informs us that he is in love with God only knows whom. And now he wants to introduce her to us, bring her home for dinner, or something.

"What is her name?" Ida asked for the sake of being polite.

Rosa Samoilovna and Semen Mikhailovich didn't even ask any questions. Who cares what her name is? Everything is crystal clear anyways.

Rosa kept silent and said nothing, even though she could have and maybe even should have said,

"You, Mulia, never even asked for your parents' advice, so why do you suddenly want to introduce your girlfriend to us?"

Semen also didn't say, even though he could have if he thought it could make any difference, "It's a good thing she is at least a Stolberg. That lady from Arkul was not even that. She was also an alter cocker, yes, terribly old, ten years older than you were."

In spite of all that, it was impossible to prevent Samuil from being happy for no reason and singing his endless songs in many different languages.

"If it's so crucial that she come here," Rosa Samoilovna finally said without looking at Samuil, "let her come."

"So who is she?" Ida asked once again.

"Don't worry, my dears!" Samuil laughed at the top of his voice. "Since you are so interested (like we could avoid being interested, Semen and Rosa thought and shrugged their shoulders) what kind of a family she is from, I can tell you that she is from a decent family."

He laughed out once again, this time because, for some reason, his long-lost Jewish accent had come out.

"Her mother is a noted engineer (Samuil could have said a lot to qualify this statement, but this was obviously not the right moment to do so), her father is also in construction, I think he works in a managerial capacity. He is a great guy, by the way. Her stepfather, Vladimir Fedorovich, is a wonderful person. He works at the Southern Railway. And my Klara has a gold medal. She is a law student, and she got accepted into law school without having to pass any exams. I can assure you," he almost whistled like he used to do in his childhood, "there is nobody else like her. And there can be nobody else. I've been hugely lucky!"

"You also had a silver medal," Rosa Samoilovna said without raising her head.

"Veiz mir," Semen Mikhailovich added.

"I knew you'd love your future daughter-in-law sight unseen," Samuil sang out, kissing everybody in turn, including Maia who'd been listening to this fascinating conversation with bated breath.

At this point, a horrible silence reigned, to use Petro Antonovich's turn of phrase.

"Oy vey," Rosa whispered, putting aside bits of cloth she'd been going over. "What daughter-in-law? Shimen, did you hear that? Put away that iron, already. Did you hear what our Mulia just said? My daughter-in-law! Oy oy oy!"

Petro Antonovich would have now repeated his favorite observation. Samuil kept smiling as he awaited further responses from his relatives.

"What does this mean?" Semen Mikhailovich asked. "What is it with all this marrying all of a sudden? You don't have two pennies to rub together!"

"Where did you find her?" Ida asked, preventing Samuil from answering the preceding question. "How come she can't wait to get married?"

Samuil had to kiss them all in turn once again. Then, he answered the last question he'd been asked,

"We've been waiting for four years, so we can both wait some more. But we are running out of patience, to be honest."

He laughed out so loudly that their neighbor, uncle Monia, dropped a glass he was holding.

And now the entire family had to sit there waiting.

"So what did they say, when are they coming?" Maia asked as she rushed into the house.

"They said nothing," Ida replied. "Their majesties will inform us in due course."

The room smelled of borscht, so Maia didn't feel disappointed.

"Well, if they don't show up today, there will be more borscht left for us," she said.

Nobody laughed at this joke, just the opposite.

"Will she bring her relatives over?" Ida enquired without visible emotions.

"Like her relatives care all that much about us," Rosa Samoilovna replied. "Every relative she has is a greser engineer. Shimen, why are you sitting there all silent? Usually, you never stop sharing your khokhme, but today you just sit there with your mouth closed and your cheeks all puffed up."

"What should I do, celebrate?" Semen Mikhailovich shrugged and looked into the window at the huge pink flowers growing out of a long stem. "A gescheft hob nicht! Mulia is bringing over his beauty. He'll have a million of such beauties in the future."

"What do you mean, a gescheft hob nicht? And what do you mean, a million?" Rosa Samoilovna was indignant. "It isn't like Mulia brings over somebody every day. Shimen, what is it that you are rambling about?"

"Is she beautiful, or something?" Maia asked.

"How should we know?" Maia snickered. "It isn't like we've ever seen her. Look at where they live and where we do."

"And where do they live?"

"In the tuches," Semen Mikhailovich answered irritably.

"Somewhere on Sumskaya Street," Ida added.

"I don't know what kind of a beauty she is," Rosa Samoilovna continued. "That's Mulia's business. We need to be hospitable to them, and then Mulia will decide for himself. Shimen, say something already. Don't just sit there all puffed up."

To this, Semen Mikhailovich would have liked to respond,

"Kisch in tuches, Rosa, why do you bother me so, why? I'm not puffed up. I just don't feel like skipping up and down the street just because Mulia is bringing somebody over."

But what's the point of saying anything if Rosa will always have a comeback, no matter what you say.

Klara, Samuil and the captain sat down underneath a salad green lampshade at a round table covered with a beige tablecloth.

"What's new onshore?" the parrot asked loudly.

The Malaysian and the Portuguese shut down his question from the very start.

"Quiet, old fool, when your superiors are talking!" yelled the irate sailors in unison.

"I'm no fool," the parrot flicked his grey feathers proudly. "At my age ("So he's grey because of age, not because of sea brine," Klara thought), I can afford not to care about hierarchies. You'd never dare to shush them," and he pointed his curved beak in the direction of Klara and Samuil. "You shush me down, though."

"Quod licet Jovi non licet bovi," noted the captain in a severe voice. Still, he smiled, and Klara thought that he must have heard this phrase from her a while ago. Or maybe he was going to hear it in the future.

"And you, my esteemed friend, have a long road to travel until you get to be a bovi ("Let alone a Jovi," Klara added.) This road is longer than the one from here to the Crimea on foot."

"I'm no spring chicken to be treated this way," rolled his "r"s the parrot in an offended voice. The only reason why he made this meaningless statement was because he wanted to have the last say.

Samuil winked at both the captain and the parrot,

"To answer the question that has been asked, things are great onshore. If they weren't, Klara and I would have never discovered you."

"If things were bad at sea, we would have never discovered you," the parrot returned the compliment. In response to strict glances from the crew, he raised his brow, shrugged his wings, and plunged into well-advised silence.

"We have a long journey ahead of us," the captain pointed at the map that was spread in front of them. It was indistinguishable from the endless, transparent window. "I would love to promise that our journey will never end but this doesn't depend just on me."

"No need to justify yourself," Klara covered his hand with hers. "Tell us, instead, where we are right now."

The captain was ready to oblige.

"Don't forget this place. I will have to return here often. Do you see the yellow and black sunflowers from my favorite poem? And those orange flowers, too? They only grow in Holland, in its very heart."

"And what is this church? It looks just like all of the churches in this area but it's still imperceptibly different."

"Everybody thinks this is a church," the captain laughed. "In reality, though, it's a tavern called "The Eleventh Commandment." There is only one tavern of this kind here in Belgium, and in Europe at large, too. The first Ten Commandments are observed in that cathedral over there. And at "The Eleventh Commandment", they serve the best dark beer in Antwerp. And that's the eleventh commandment."

"I wonder why these mugs have four handles," Samuil said as he remembered the pub on Sverdlov Street, right in front the fire lookout tower, where there was often a shortage of glasses.

"Belgian stout is never diluted with water," the captain said because he also remembered that bar on Sverdlov Street, "otherwise it will turn into a lager, and that's a completely different thing in every respect. Of course, as we know from experience, finding a handle after a second mug of undiluted stout becomes problematic. The more handles there are, the easier it is to find one of them."

Klara put her mug aside carefully, and they took a seat in a tram in Hannover. Dusk had fallen over Germany, lights went on in the tram. A big group of locals was sitting in front of them. They looked very much like the one Zinovi had told Klara about but they were happy and joyful thanks to an open and half-consumed bottle of champagne. They embraced each other, swayed, and sang an ancient sad song. At the next stop, two giants entered the tram. They were panting and trying not to stumble on the hopelessly high steps. Samuil was sure he had seen them somewhere before. Probably it was at the Blagoveschensky marketplace or inside that same bar on Sverdlov Street. The beer might have been diluted but not with water because the giants had a heavy, harsh and attentive stare. When they managed to get their eyes into focus in the same way as you catch an escaping cat by the tail, they looked at the strangers who were singing in an unacceptably foreign language, embraced each other, and bellowed "The Moscow Nights." They sang the song so loudly that the tram had to make an effort to stay on track. The hosts first froze in terror but immediately arrived at the only acceptable solution and joined in the song, which they sang almost without mistakes.

"It sometimes happens", Klara smiled, "that a small difference in the details only reinforces the basic similarity."

"Does everybody know this song in Europe?" the Malaysian and the Portuguese sailors asked.

"Of course. Even though it hasn't been written yet," the parrot murmured under his salty breath.

Klara stared at the Saint Lawrence River that was as wide as the Dnieper in Rechitsa. It was flowing energetically into the Atlantic.

"We seem to be very far away from your native land?" Klara asked the captain, Samuil, and herself.

"Madame," the captain kissed her hand, "this land is much more native to us than might seem at a first glance."

Then, much later, so late that Klara and Samuil probably didn't even hear him, he said,

"As it turns out, every land is equally strange and native at the same time. The place where you weigh your anchor is as important as the one where you cast it."

"Let's not hurry the time," the Portuguese sailor sighed and looked with sadness at his beloved Archipelago of the Azores. "Unfortunately ("Or fortunately," the Malaysian added), it makes no sense to do so. Everything will come to pass whenever it's time for it to do so. The islands we just passed are proof of that."

Klara waved at her from the dusty road that curled like her hair, and Klara waved her good-bye for a little while. She was looking downwards, at herself, Klara, Isaak, and their companions who were walking from Rechitsa to a far-away synagogue located about ten kilometers away from Toledo. They were walking tirelessly and slowly because hurrying and feeling tired was impossible on a Saturday morning.

They walked on, across Ukraine and Byelorussia, Germany and Belgium, across Holland that was as homey as all the other countries they had crossed. Klara could see them very well from above: the captain of their ship, she and Samuil right next to him, Maria, Mila, still looking like Sancho but a beautiful and thin one, Vladimir Fedorovich, Zinovi, Berta, and even (this "even" sounded really funny and silly!) the Rose-Fingered Maiden, and even (this "even" is too funny for words, really!) Petro Antonovich, Samuil's Vice-Chancellor, Professor Fuks, Professor Katsnelson, Plevako, Alexander Blekhman, Vertinsky, the Feldmans, and – "may the devil take them!" smiles Vladimir Fedorovich – Strelkina, Volkova and Pipa.

They were all walking down that road, and without at least one of them, this entire road would not exist. Just like their Blagoveschensky Cathedral would not exist without the far-away synagogue in Toledo, the house at 82 Sumskaya Street would not be there if it weren't for the hills around Toledo, and this ship would not come into existence without the Seminary Hill.

On top of the hill and behind it, the forties were drawing to a close.

The centuries and the decades tangled like Klara's hair on the amazing dusty road that led them from Toledo to a far-away synagogue. They joined each other and separated and then flowed all over the world like the Saint Lawrence River. On top of the hill and behind it, fluff was soaring in the form of weightless marshmallows and snow-white butterflies, the leaves fell from Kharkov's chestnut-trees, and the Portuguese sailor soundlessly addressed Klara, playfully rolling his "r"s,

"Unfortunately, Madame, the leaves are falling from the trees. Isn't it time for you to go back?"

She didn't feel like responding, but the Malaysian approached them and reminded her with a bow, rolling his "r"s in the same way,

"This is Singapore, the city of lions, Maestro's last song, and the final destination of your journey."

King George, whose number did not reflect his importance, nodded from his corner without looking very sad and straightened his crown that kept slipping off,

"Fortunately, it's time for you to go back."

Klara placed the book with mother-of-pearl covers back in the book-case, right next to the book that the captain used to take out more often than any other. Then, she took Samuil by the hand and asked the captain by way of good-bye, or, as she preferred to hope, just the opposite,

"Have you been to all these countries?"

"I'm sure I will," the captain promised. "Directly or indirectly, Madame, I will get there. Just wait and see."

"Shall we see?" Klara glanced at Samuil.

He nodded and kissed her, even though he wasn't completely sure.

"I'm sure I will," the captain smiled. "And I promise that I will take you with me."

The Portuguese and the Malayan sighed, and the parrot felt so sad that he had to close his eyes to avoid crying like a veritable spring chicken.

The city of lemon and banana trees disappeared before ever having time to appear. The tigers and the lions at the

Kharkov zoo howled in their cages, as if they had heard people talking about them. Their howling drowned out the artist's last song, and the grey parrot yelped in fear. Vertinsky was so overwhelmed and stricken that he shrugged his shoulders and rolled his "r"s in what Vladimir Fedorovich would call a desperate way to address the audience,

"My modest baritone cannot compete with the bassos of the tsars and the kings of nature."

Klara, Samuil and everybody else had to wait for almost an eternity until the irate tsars calmed down. Then, he resumed singing, and none of his songs, fortunately, turned out to be the last.

He continued singing until it became very light inside the summer theater and very dark in their immense world.

LVI

"Why do these simple folks always have so many relatives?" asked Maria in a way that made it obvious she required no answer. Then she swallowed a spoonful of soup and made a face that could force one to think that the soup had gone bad (as if Klara would ever allow any food to spoil or burn).

"The simpler a person is," Maria continued, "the more relatives he has. Relatives are like acne. Only you can never get rid of them, no matter what you try. Besides, nobody even tries."

Vladimir Fedorovich kept eating the soup with his usual appetite.

"What is so unusual about this?" he shrugged his shoulders. "There are small families, and then there are big ones. Why should we care when we have a family of our own, thank God?"

Klara didn't want to take either side although she had already almost formed an opinion sight unseen.

"Petkevich, see the writing on the wall already," Maria said ("which wall would that be?" Vladimir Fedorovich wondered in silence). "Family and relatives are two completely different things. Relatives, just so you know, have nothing to do with family. And it would be great if our family had nothing to do with them.

She finished her soup, nodded her thanks to Klara, and temporarily concluded as Klara handed out the second course,

"A relative is just an empty word, Petkevich. Family, however, is reality."

"Oh God," Vladimir Fedorovich murmured, "Samuil finally wants to introduce Klara to his family. Good for him. They haven't seen her once in these five years, so let them meet her already," he smiled at Klara in the same way as he used to when she would tell him about the king looking just like the tsar.

The stew that Klara prepared was even better than usual, so he was physically incapable of arguing. In any case, Vladimir Fedorovich disliked arguing and considered it a wrong thing to do. If a person thinks something, let him. Why interfere with that? Why try to prevent a person from enjoying a thought of their own here and there?

"They haven't been together for five years," Maria clarified in a severe voice. "Just four." (Vladimir Fedorovich kept silent, and so did Klara.) "If they've waited for four years, they could wait for another twenty-four."

"Klara," she addressed her daughter, seeing her smile, "why are you so silent? I just started getting used to your Samuil, and now his relatives have to come into the picture all of a sudden. Why do you have to do go all the way to that Kasrilovka of theirs just to meet them?"

"Why Kasrilovka?" Vladimir Fedorovich asked. "They live in Balashovka, it's half an hour from here by tram. An hour, at most. In any case, they live closer to us than to Rechitsa."

Klara appreciated this brave statement, but Maria was invincible and unmovable.

"Petkevich," she snickered with condescension ("what is there to be expected from an ignoramus?"), "have you ever even been to Rechitsa? Of course, your favorite tram isn't there, but there are no relatives there either, thank God."

I could have objected (objected to Maria?) that she had crowds of relatives in Rechitsa. She hasn't visited Balashovka while I've been there once. I went there for work, to inspect the depot. To be honest, deep inside I agreed that it was no place for Klara. At most, she should go this one time to see what it is all about.

"Thank you very much," Vladimir Fedorovich said and made a very silly suggestion, like he usually does, what's the matter with him, really, "Klara, maybe it will be best if Samuil brings them over to meet us?"

"What did you just say???" Maria slowly got up from the table. "We should let half of Balashovka's population inside our apartment?? Are you out of your mind, Petkevich???"

Klara rushed to kiss her and calm her down,

"Mama, let's not erect barricades between Sumskaya and Dobrokhotova Streets. Nothing bad will happen if I visit the relatives' den. I won't lose anything if I go there. Maybe I will even end up gaining some."

"What can you possibly gain from visiting these losers?" Maria frowned and sat down.

"Samuil will start loving me even more," Klara laughed, even though she hoped that the degree of Samuil's love for her was never going to depend on relatives. To be honest, I didn't really feel like laughing.

This encounter was as necessary as a visit to a dentist's. Klara had started preparing for it psychologically as soon as Samuil proposed for the first time, or maybe even before that. In any case, one could put up with it just this once because if you manage to suffer through it just once – no more than that! – then you'll never get another tooth-ache again.

"Senia," she asked Samuil a couple of days before their visit to Dobrokhotova, "even though you have a different specialization as a doctor, you still probably know the answer. What does it feel to have somebody drill a healthy tooth?"

Samuil nodded in amazement,

"I was really afraid that my wife would turn out to be a sadist."

"It isn't too late to change your mind," Klara smiled.

"It has been too late for a long time," Samuil sighed. "It's been too late for over four years now."

That was when Klara made her final decision to get her healthy teeth drilled.

LVII

In reality, it took them a long time to set the date. They weren't going to get married before Klara's last year of law school, which was going to be the fifth year. Klara knew that for sure, even though Samuil never really understood it. In any case, it took two to reach an agreement, which Samuil and Klara knew very well, so he tried hard to do his part.

Winter wasn't going to work because New Year's was celebrated in December and Klara's birthday was in January. As Klara said, she wasn't up to so much partying. Besides, she had her final exams. This wasn't something to celebrate but it was more important than any celebration. February is a sad little month that is not only too short but is also known for its really horrible weather. As Vladimir Fedorovich says, the winds get desperate in February. Klara knew that even she was not going to be able to overcome both the winter storms and the wedding. Forget the "even", she simply wasn't going to be able to do it.

Spring wasn't good either. On March 8th, the International Women's Day was celebrated. Men feel subservient on this day, and a subservient man is as bad as a servile woman. Even no man at all is better than that. April is as bad as January because Samuil has his birthday, on the same day as Lenin did. May is full of holidays, one better and more important than other, and then one needs to prepare for the exams.

Summer is really bad for a wedding. In June, she has her finals, while July and August should be reserved for resting and not for getting married. Besides, as Vladimir Fedorovich says, the heat gets desperate in summer. Nobody can get married in such circumstances, agreed? Of course, he did his part and agreed.

So how about the fall then? OK, let's think about it. The school year starts in September. Nobody gets married at the start of a school year. There are two more birthdays coming in September, her mother's and Vladimir Fedorovich's. And in November they will be celebrating the anniversary of the October Revolution and her father's birthday.

October is all that's left. It was one of Klara's two favorite months. Of course, she loved all of them, albeit in different ways. May was the best of all, but she liked October, too. It wasn't as ecstatic and elated as May. The white, purple and pink trees and bushes were not in bloom. The thunderstorms that were never scary weren't succeeded by the sun that looked like a polished coin and winked happily at passersby. The summer rain didn't patter over the roofs of Kharkov, the roofs that were so incredibly tall that one could have never torn a T-shirt on them.

October was different. October and May did not resemble each other. They were like the sea that hid behind the mountains of the Crimea. In this sense, they were both parts of some incomprehensible whole. Just like force of will and peace constituted a whole, that very whole that was called happiness.

And October was not limited to all the yellows, reds and browns in the Shevchenko Gardens, in the little square behind the Glass Fountain, and in the Gorky Park. It didn't consist only of the sad, slightly tart smell of the quiet streets of the city. There was more to it than the ticklish, caressing threads of sunlight. And there was more than the sun that was still red hot, especially at the end of a day that would simply refuse to run out, but that was not the careless sun of May. In October, the sun would be slow, pondering, deep in thought, enriched with mysterious far-away knowledge.

October in Kharkov is that most endless time of the endless year when everything is quiet and peaceful. You can kick at the heap of the fallen leaves, take Samuil by the hand and smile as you watch the weightless October leaves covered with red veins float to the ground. The leaves cover the dreamy alley to protect it from the rains of November.

And then Samuil gives me a kiss and probably guesses what I was thinking about because he was thinking the same thing.

And then Klara gave me a kiss and repeated the same words that I had just been thinking in silence.

LVIII

Rosa Samoilovna's frozen smile reminded Klara of a pattern of frost on a window in January.

"Please come in," she enunciated.

How could Klara refuse to please her?

"It took you a while to get here?" Ida snickered. "Have you been traveling from the Far East or something?"

"East-schmeast," Rosa Samoilovna said softly. "We do live far away. I'm sorry for the trouble. Please come in, take a seat, Mulia."

"Mila, I knew that the Far East was far away," Klara smiled. "I just didn't know it was so far."

Mila giggled,

"You, Stolberg, are a subjective idealist. The Far East isn't far from Kharkov. It's the other way round."

Samuil joined in sympathetically, "According to this statement of yours and Klara's descriptions of you, you are as much of a subjective idealist as she is. And it suits you well."

"Once again, it's the other way round," Mila disagreed. "I'm not a subjective one, like Stolberg. Klara is more subjective than even Maria Isaakovna herself. I, however, am even more objective than my Aunt Basia."

"Sancho Panza also used to enjoy arguing with Don Quixote," Maria Isaakovna observed.

Mila nodded with satisfaction, "He was right in doing that because, otherwise, Don Quixote would have lost his qualifications. What kind of Don Quixote can you have without a Sancho? He'd be like a horseman without the organ he really needs to sit on a horse."

Clouds gathered over Balashovka. They tried to control themselves but failed, so they either sprinkled or wrinkled.

"We are a little cramped here," Rosa Samoilovna said. "Sorry for that."

"We don't mind that at all," Samuil said with a complete lack of originality. "Why should we mind? Klara, meet Rosa Samoilovna, Semen Mikhailovich, Ida and Maia. You've heard me speak of them a lot."

"Klara," said Klara.

Klara smiled at her imperceptibly. She also smiled at the thought that she was Klara, too. Why "too", anyways?

"All that's missing is that we start figuring out which ones among you matter more than others," Mila whispered in a way that made clear she wasn't upset with Klara. "We'll keep figuring it out until we are soaked through."

They could neither here nor feel the rain. It descended upon them slowly and quietly, like a new snow descending on the roofs of Sumskaya Street.

"So do you live on Sumskaya Street?" Maia asked.

"Yes, close to Dzerzhinsky Square," Klara answered. "Before the war, we lived in Pushkin Entry, but that apartment was taken away."

"Where do you study?" Semen Mikhailovich asked, serving himself some latkes.

"Let's stop these formalities already", Ida suggested and served latkes to Maia and herself.

"Step under the umbrella, ladies," invited them the captain who had disembarked just in time. "It is smallish and quite sufficient for all of us."

"Thank you so very much," Vladimir Fedorovich smiled. "All of us are never numerous, thank God."

"Imagine this," Zinovi sighed. *"We barely managed to turn around when the umbrella logically passed from them to us. In any case, there is enough space for all of us here, as promised."*

"Of course, we can dispense with formalities," Klara agreed. "I'm in law school."

"You will be a lawyer?" Maia asked. "Mulia told us."

Samuil nodded and served latkes to Klara, Rosa Samoilovna, and himself.

"I hope so," Klara said. "If I manage to pass the exams and graduate, that is."

"That's good. We will have our own lawyer if something should happen," Ida sneered.

"I wonder what could happen," Rosa Samoilovna shrugged without raising her head. "Sei gesund. I'm not sure if you like latkes, though."

"Thank you so very much," Vladimir Fedorovich nodded. "I like potato pancakes a lot."

"Especially the ones that have a crust. Like these ones," Zinovi clarified.

"Make sure you don't get too crusty, Ziama. Or you'll be like one of those crusty figures of authority", Vladimir Fedorovich warned.

Zinovi disagreed,

"For your information, Volodia, if it crunches, you can use it in a crunch. And those authority figures can go on crunching their numbers."

"Let's postpone the official evaluation of everybody present," the captain suggested. "I think the more we postpone it, the better for all of us."

"You see, Senia," Klara said with her Rechitsa smile, "and people always told me that youth is unreliable."

"You probably read a lot?" Ida asked.

"Our Muila also has to read all the time," Rosa Samoilovna remarked in an uninflected voice.

Samuil laughed and kissed Klara's hand, "I'll never be able to read as much as Klara does. And even if I force myself to do it, I'll still retain nothing. But I can promise that I'm also quite OK in every possible respect."

His laughter could be heard down the entire Dobrokhotova Street, which made Uncle Monia break yet another glass. Klara gave Samuil an imaginary kiss on the cheek.

"*The more you read,*" Mila elaborated on his idea, "*the more you forget. The best way to improve your memory is to read nothing. This way you'll have a chance to retain something. Little by little, you'll end up with a good memory.*"

"Maybe I should try your method of memory improvement," Samuil mused. "I'm fed up with reading. It's time to start doing something in life."

"*Mila is no specialist in memory improvement,*" Maria Isaakovna *declared a bitter and self-evident truth.*

Mila was unruffled.

"*There are obligations that I fulfill unfailingly,*" *she said.* "*To give just one example...*"

"Mulia was always a role model," Rosa Samoilovna said. She avoided looking at those present. Most of all, she avoided looking at Klara. "He isn't some schmuck, like they all are nowadays."

"Az och und vey, are schmucks in fashion today, what?" Semen Mikhailovich murmured under his breath. "Why say such things if they make no sense, why?"

Rosa Samoilovna wanted to give him an answer he deserved, but Klara didn't give her a chance, "Semen Mikhailovich, do you work at a factory?"

"Yes, I am a painter. I work at the bicycle factory," Semen Mikhailovich answered.

"So why did you decide to go to law school?" the captain interjected just in time. "Didn't you always prefer literature? You even look more like a philologist than an attorney."

"I look like an attorney, too," Klara welcomed his interest. "I didn't really like the philology crowd. Even I get influenced by the surroundings, you know? Besides... What can I say about literature that will be of any value? I love reading, not writing about what I've read. I'd even say that it's best to keep silent about what you've read or you run the risk of making your interlocutor uncomfortable by letting him express the silly idea he is dying to share."

The captain mused for a while and then asked...

"And how about you, Ida?"

"I work at the soap factory."

"Mommy brings home animals!" Maia boasted.

The animals stood on the cupboard. They were colorful, red and blue, and smelled of soap, unlike the seven ivory elephants.

The captain asked in an uncertain voice, "How will it make you feel if..."

Klara wanted to encourage him to continue, but Samuil said firmly,

"If you want my opinion, don't pay too much attention to this issue."

"Mulia," Rosa Samoilovna said very quietly, almost without opening her mouth, "you can take my portion of food."

Captain kept silent for a while, but then he finally responded to Klara and Samuil and to himself, "I know what you mean. I have an excuse, though. This book is the excuse for literature. Literature would be too risky an enterprise without it. Or maybe it would just be a useless one. Like these pink long-stemmed flowers would make no sense if it weren't for the window that allows Semen Mikhailovich to see them."

Semen Mikhailovich was looking out of the window at the washed out pink flowers whose stems looked like stilts and thinking that the most important things were probably out there instead of in here. Here, everything was about to end. So be it, there is nothing anybody can do, especially not if one tries. Rosa doesn't understand this. She wanted to do what's best, which is why she said so quietly, almost without opening her mouth, in a way that it was impossible not to hear her, "Mulia, you can take my portion of food."

Klara and Samuil were walking towards the tram stop, and Klara held his hand.

"Senia," she said, looking straight ahead, "do you want us to be together?"

"Of course, my love," Samuil said unhappily. "Do you?"

"I still do. And if you want this "still" to last, make sure you give me a chance to love your relatives *in absentia*. And I will do everything in my power to let you love them *in praesentia*. You never need to doubt me."

Of course, I accepted this constructive offer, especially since I had no choice.

LIX

"What's the need to get married so out of the blue?" Maria Isaakovna shrugged her shoulders in a decisive manner. "Pipa, close the door on the outside, please. You can take my pan off the stove if it gets in your way so much. Put it on the windowsill. I'll collect it later. This Pipa can even drive a healthy male to a heart attack, may she rot in hell."

"Mama, are you ready to hear the answer?" Klara asked with a smile.

Vladimir Fedorovich also smiled though didn't stop reading the newspaper. Samuil, however, felt even less like smiling than Maria Isaakovna, albeit his reasons for that were the exact opposite.

"Of course," Maria Isaakovna continued, "you now know how to justify anything. This Professor Fuks, may he always feel as joyous as I do right now, taught you to prove what cannot be proven. You, Samuil, are a grown man (here Samuil sighed deeply but imperceptibly). Can you tell me why you are both in such a hurry to go and get married all of a sudden, as Pipa would say? Is this some new fashion, or something?"

Samuil blushed violently,

"Maria Isaakovna, what do you mean, all of a sudden? Klara and I have been dating forever. It's time we took the plunge and put an end to this whole thing."

"Marriage, Samuil, does not put an end to anything, just so you know. I know from experience that it doesn't even offer a small break. Petkevich, will you say something already? If you have anything to say, that is. What kind of person are you? How can you hide behind your newspaper when such an important matter is being discussed?"

"Maria," Vladimir Fedorovich responded peaceably, trying, as usual, to quell the fighting and restore peace and quiet, "everything is fantastic. Do we have anything against Samuil? How can anybody have anything against him? In any case, all that matters is that Klara has nothing against him. Everything is fine, everybody is happy, so be it. Who needs all these discussions?"

"My love, do you have anything against me?" Samuil asked Klara, allowing himself to smile.

"I have no idea," Klara responded. "First, let's get married, and then we'll see how it goes."

Maria Isaakovna shrugged her shoulders again,

"Who cares if she has or she hasn't. Maybe Samuil, too, has something against me (Samuil's face acquired an imperceptible greenish tinge). But what matters is that we make a principled decision. What's so hard to understand?"

"Mama," Klara interjected, "what do you mean by "too"? Isn't that where the crux of the problem still lies?"

"Please stop picking on my words. Was it Fuks who taught you to disrespect your parents and pick on your mother? Too or not too, who cares? I'm asking you why you are in such a rush when we are talking about a very important issue."

Vladimir Fedorovich smiled, and this time, Maria could see this smile through the newspaper sheet.

"Volodia," she raised her voice even though it was quite high already. "Why do you keep hiding behind your newspaper and making faces at me? How can you even compare? Today everything is different from how it was back then."

"Oh God," Vladimir Fedorovich tried explaining himself inoffensively. "I'm not making anything. You are the only one who makes things around here. They've been dating for so long

("And fruitlessly, too!" Klara added) that other people could have already gotten married, divorced, acquainted with a ton of useful and useless people, acquired a house in Massandra, and married once again."

"What house? Why Massandra?" Maria Isaakovna exclaimed. "This man will go crazy and drive me crazy, too. Who can afford to go around buying houses in Massandra?"

"Mama, this was just a metaphor Vladimir Fedorovich used to make his point," Klara said in an attempt to calm her down. "Vladimir Fedorovich is saying that it is easier for some people to buy a house in Massandra than it is for others to do something as natural as getting married."

"I have no idea what you are talking about," Maria Isaakovna waved them off. "Just remember that if you don't get straight A's on your finals, you will not graduate with Honors. Then you will only have yourself to blame."

Klara laughed and kissed her,

"Mama, can you really imagine me not getting straight A's? Do you really believe that might happen? It's easier to believe in buying a house in Massandra, in my opinion."

Nobody believed it, of course, and Maria Isaakovna believed it least of all. For her daughter to fail to graduate with Honors?

"Besides," Klara added agreeably though seriously, "you said yourself that I'm a real attorney now. And a real attorney should be able to marry whomever she wishes. As a person whose job it is to protect law and order, I cannot live a life of depravity and sin, can I?"

Maria's big eyes bulged out and became huge. The newspaper stopped rustling. Even the bust in the book-case looked like it was listening in.

"What?" Maria Isaakovna either inhaled or exhaled. "What did you just say? What do you mean, a life of depravity and sin?"

Samuil felt himself becoming covered in spots. Klara evaluated the situation and laughed as loudly as she used to when she and Mila walked down Chernyshevskaya Street.

"Mama," she said after a few minutes of laughter that to Maria Isaakovna seemed quite unhealthy, "when I mentioned sin, I was only referring to the fact that we still lack an official document, that's all. Just look at us. Don't you see that we, alas, are an embodiment of pure thoughts and unblemished morality? Pipa, just eat this miserable soup already, if you want it so much. I'll make more later. I only hope you won't eat that new soup as well."

And she laughed so loudly that everybody, even Maria Isaakovna felt the need to join, while Uncle Monia probably was left without a single good glass.

LX

Leaves were falling and arranging themselves in an October carpet that had been missing from their regional courthouse where marriages were celebrated. It was located close to Klara's house, at the corner of Chernyshevskaya Street, the same place where Samuil had seen her for the very first time and she had failed to see him for the very last.

Maria Isaakovna and Vladimir Fedorovich stood to the side of the bride and the groom. Zinovi and Berta stood opposite them. There were also other guests whom Maria failed to notice. She hadn't seen Zinovi since leaving him, and now she was avoiding having to look at him once again. She looked at Klara and felt like crying, even though she never cried.

During the war, at the Dnieper, in college, as a single mother, at the uranium mines, on her business trips – never did she feel the slightest desire to cry or even to feel momentarily sorry for herself. She had neither time nor the need for that. Even now she had no desire to cry, which made avoiding it even harder. She watched Klara put her signature on the marriage certificate, kiss Samuil, place a ring on his finger and get a similar but bigger ring placed on her own finger. The room felt small and stuffy, and it kept getting smaller and stuffier. Maria felt boxed in by its walls.

Then, the woman conducting the ceremony made an announcement, and the crowd erupted in the kind of noise she'd only heard when the end of the construction of the station on Lake

Sevan was announced. She kissed Klara and probably Samuil, too, and they all emerged into the street. Klara was walking with Samuil, Maria and Vladimir Fedorovich followed. Petkevich must have been smiling and feeling happy about everything, as usual, but at this point, she neither noticed nor cared.

They had a short way to walk back, but it felt like a very long road. Maria walked without noticing the city around her. Basseinaya Street stretched out to an extreme length. It took forever to turn the corner, and walking from the corner to their building took even longer. Instead of crying or wishing something good to the bride and groom, Maria suddenly thought that her age – forty-one – was half of the number of their building which was eighty-two. In forty-one more years, she will reach the building's number and they will both be eighty-two. That meant there was very little time remaining.

What she needed was to gain a foothold. This expression sounded trite and simplistic, but there was nobody to suggest a better one. Nobody ever offered her any suggestions. People either asked for her advice or allowed her to suggest things to them. Now, however. . . She needed something that she could think about and feel secure and happy, like she used to feel before.

What was it that made her feel this way before, she wondered as they walked past the grocery store on Sumskaya Street. What was it?

Was it walking from Sumskaya Street to Dzerzhinsky Square every morning? Was it her unhurried journey to design yet another power station? Or was it having that balcony on the fourth floor? The balcony that was so high up that she could see the entire city of Kharkov from it?

She looked at their balcony and noticed how hopelessly empty and useless it looked, just like the courthouse on Basseinaya Street they were coming from. It was simply there, and nobody cared whether it was or wasn't.

And suddenly she found her answer. This was something that could only take place all of a sudden and only if one kept searching for it patiently and hopefully, without getting desperate even if the answer took a while to emerge. She even stopped, or maybe she started to walk faster, who cares? That didn't matter anymore. She had gotten her answer, and everything regained meaning once again, Kharkov, their building, their balcony, and even the courthouse.

When Maria got her answer, she burst out laughing for the first time in her life. It wasn't just any laughter because she'd had a lot of that in her life. There was nothing unusual about that kind of regular laughter. She was no killjoy or anything like that. But such an outburst of glee or relief was something she experienced for the first time.

She turned to Klara and Samuil, or maybe she caught up with them. Who cares, anyways? What does it really matter? They couldn't believe their eyes and ears when she asked them, or rather, told them because it was more important for her to understand and to tell them, but to ask was important, too. And then she felt so free and peaceful that it reminded her of the time when she had crossed the Dnieper, come back home, and her mother called her to dinner.

She asked the question when Klara and Samuil were walking from the courthouse, laughing so loud that the entire street could hear them and Vladimir Fedorovich felt happy listening to them.

"We are lucky that she didn't ask us to kiss in public," Klara observed. "She's lucky she didn't, too."

"Darling, the woman was at work. It wasn't up to her to ask us that," Samuil elaborated on her thought. "Only our relatives and the guests at the wedding can ask the bride and the groom to exchange a kiss."

"Our relatives and the guests at the wedding are the same thing," Klara continued. "If you are being exhorted to exchange a kiss, it's the content of the exhortation and not the status of the person exhorting you that matters."

"One needs to be a relative of yours to commit the error of arguing with you. Thank God, a husband is not a relative. And also thank God that the poor woman did not let us down and only suggested we could exchange a kiss if we wanted to, instead of asking us to do so."

"Exactly. We were given a choice of whether we wanted to exchange it or not. And in case we didn't. . ."

"What do you mean, we didn't?" Samuil exclaimed.

"Of course, we did, but it was our personal business whether we were going to do it. We were not going to kiss just because somebody told us to. Have you noticed how she referred to us as a young couple? What would she call us if we were ninety years old? Would she really say we were an old couple?"

"If we managed to get ourselves to the marriage ceremony, we must be young," Samuil chimed in.

"It would be great if we remained of the same sound mind at that age as we were when we got married."

Klara paused for a moment and quoted,

"'Though this be madness. . .'"

Then she added,

"Senia, what if at the age of ninety, you find yourself in the grip of senile psychosis and start attacking me? My only consolation is that at ninety you will not pose much of a threat."

"My love, whenever and however I go mad, you will only feel better and better by my side," Samuil reassured her.

And he gave Klara the kind of look that made it very clear to the passersby they had no need of exhorting them to kiss.

Maria Isaakovna, however, helped the passersby out, leaving Klara amazed with the depths that her mother had managed to glimpse.

"Mama, this matter can only be resolved at home and in a while, too. We can't do it in the middle of the street, don't you agree?"

LXI

"Take a seat, darling," Zinovi said. "Standing makes no sense. Although, in some cases, sitting doesn't, either"

"It isn't just standing that keeps having no sense," Klara answered gaily as she sat down on the sofa and took a bite out of a huge white apple that had been eagerly awaiting her arrival in the same newish vase. "Where is your fatherly blessing, anyway? Your daughter made a good marriage and is entitled to hear her wise father deliver wise speeches."

"I've been wondering what this attractive twenty-one-year-old Rose-Fingered Maiden was doing in such a hurry. It turns out that the answer is both simple and hard at the same time. She was hurrying to get married."

Zinovi kissed her and emitted the same kind of sigh that he used to share with Petro Antonovich when discussing a similar topic,

"The younger generation doesn't make us wait."

Unexpectedly for Klara, he recited,

"Oh youth, oh innocence,
You have abandoned me for good."

He didn't look in the least sad, just the opposite, which was why Klara didn't allow his prosaic words to distract her.

"Dad, have you been to the library?"

Zinovi assumed a mysterious and distant look, approached the book-case with a slower stride as usual, and took out two smallish similar-looking books in light-blue hard covers.

"Benediktov?!" Klara exclaimed. "Dad, have you robbed the library?"

Zinovi handed her the books and gave her another kiss,

"Berta and I have been to Tallinn for our honeymoon. We went into a used book store, and I suddenly saw these books by Benediktov. Both volumes were published by Wolf and Co. Mind you, they were published in 1902 and not in 1909. As we can see, anybody can make a mistake. It's the same year when I was born, not your mother."

Klara opened one of the volumes on a random page and read aloud,

"You often find your entrance barred
Where others easily go in.
For you, however, somehow
There is no place within."

"Dad," she asked with a slightly dazed look as she leafed through the volume, "how do you manage to do this?"

"This is my wedding gift for you," Zinovi said contentedly. "And may you, Samuil, and your future son or daughter. . ."

"Son," Klara said without putting the book aside.

"May all of you never find your entrance barred. Just try to choose untrodden paths. The trodden ones are covered with the footsteps of others."

"Agreed. They are also very crowded. And crowds are no place for me anyways."

Zinovi smiled,

"This depends on what kind of crowd we are talking about and whether we are discussing its quality and its quantity."

Klara sighed,

"I'm afraid a crowd is always low-quality. It's one of those cases that illustrate the principle of dialectics: quantity hopelessly and irreparably translates into quality. One can be happy anywhere with the person one loves, of course, but I'm not yet ready for just anywhere."

"What are you ready for, my dear?" Zinovi asked with an unperturbed curiosity.

"I'm ready for precisely where I am right now, in every sense of the word, Dad."

Klara laughed and kissed Zinovi's cheeks so loudly that they surprised both him and her by clinking.

She sighed wistfully and added,

"And when we have the son..."

Klara didn't finish. For now, she only could think about it but not to talk.

She started to think about the most important thing while Klara – right now, at this very moment, looked in on them from her backyard in Rechitsa. When she saw that Klara was deep in thought, she decided not to disturb her, closed the gate quietly, and went back home to Isaak.

LXII

"Mama, such things don't happen all of a sudden," Klara answered peaceably. "I've made my decision a while ago, and Senia happens to agree with me. Do you agree, Senia?"

Samuil laughed,

"Klarochka, I agree with you for two reasons. One, because I'm smart (the entire communal apartment must have heard his laughter.) And two, because you are right."

Klara nodded benevolently,

"Your second statement proves that the first one was true. The fact that I'm right still comes first, though."

"Oh God, who cares anyways?" Vladimir Fedorovich asked. "What matters is that the baby must be healthy. What he is to be called is the last thing we should be thinking about."

"Petkevich," Maria Isaakovna exclaimed in indignation, "why do you always have to contradict me? You have this habit of contradicting whatever I say whenever I say it."

She turned away from Vladimir Fedorovich and addressed Klara once again,

"Just tell me what you have against Isaak. How is that a bad name for the baby? Can you explain that?"

Klara had to put aside Roman law for a moment, but only for a moment because she was going to have her final exam in Professor Fuks's class very soon.

"Mama," she said firmly, "how do you imagine his full name? Isaak Samoilovich Blekhman? Seriously? Don't get upset, please. Try to remain calm for a moment ("Calm? How can I remain calm when something so important is being discussed?") and think about it. Can my son be called Isaak Samoilovich?"

Maria pretended to think,

"I wonder what you'd say if he wasn't Samoilovich but Ivanovich or maybe even Vasilievich. Then what?"

"Are you trying to say that I could have married some unknown Vasia? As Mila's Aunt Basia used to say, can your daughter really be interpreted this way?"

Maria Isaakovna still refused to consider herself beaten,

"Sweetheart, it has been traditional to name a baby, fine, a son, why do you keep picking on me? To name a son after his grandfather. Your grandfather, may he rest in peace, was called Isaak. So what's wrong with calling your son Isaak, as well? I named you Klara, didn't I? Even though I wanted to name you Elena."

"And I like the name Victor," Samuil announced in a way that still sounded unexpected to Maria Isaakovna. "Let's forget the grandfathers, may they rest in eternity. The kid will have a life of his own. Today, we know all about the grandfather, the grandmother, and all the relatives. Nobody will ask him what his grandfather's name is, don't you think? They'll ask him, "Blekhman, what's your first name?"

And he'll say,

"Victor."

It sounds beautiful and manly."

"Samuil, how can you object to the name of Isaak," Maria Isaakovna inquired indignantly, "when you are no Victor yourself. Aren't you a Samuil?"

"I wouldn't mind being a Victor. Only nobody asked my opinion. My mother insisted I should be called Mulia, like some salesgirl in a kiosk. If they'd asked my advice, though, I'd have suggested a serious manly name."

Klara was not entirely convinced.

"Victor sounds quite good, I even like it. But the diminutives are horrible. Vitia, Vityunia, or even Vityok? No, I won't be able to deal with Vityok. This is out of the question."

"Nothing is good enough for you," Maria Isaakovna waved her off. "With your contrariness, it's a good thing you decided to become a lawyer. No matter what anyone says, you can always find an objection. I have no idea who you are taking after."

Everybody had an idea but avoided saying anything for that very reason. Samuil suddenly experienced a flash of brilliance.

"Listen," he exclaimed and slapped his forehead, "how is a great-grandfather worse than a grandfather?"

Those present failed to object to his words and, instead, gave him a long, hard stare, while Klara thought,

"If we have reached the stage of great-grandfathers, I can only imagine. . . If grandfather's name is Isaak, who's to say that great-grandfather's isn't Srul?"

"My father is called Semen Mikhailovich", Samuil went on. "So let's call our son Mikhail!"

It became deathly quiet, after which all of them – Klara, Vladimir Fedorovich, and even, as shocking as it might sound, Maria Isaakovna – nodded, thought it over, and then nodded once again.

"Mikhail means we'll call him Misha for short," Klara mused. "Sounds good. Listen, everybody, I think I might like it!"

"What do you mean, you think?" Maria Isaakovna asked. "If even Mikhail is no good for you, then, to be honest, I have no idea what more you need. Shall we leave the kid without a name, like the nameless soldier?"

Klara paused as she repeated to herself both the name and all the possible diminutives. Then, she finally said,

"I'll think about it."

And she went back to her desk to prepare for her final in Roman law.

LXIII

The elevator thumped its floor and clanged its door, as usual. Samuil jumped into their room without even taking off his shoes. There was no time for that. Besides, who could think about such trivial details at a moment like this? He'd spent the entire endless night and the entire endless morning at the maternity ward. And only when he'd become desperate and had been waiting for God knew how long and was prepared to wait for much longer just to make sure that they were both fine, the nurse finally emerged like the sea emerges from behind the Crimea mountains, like Klara had emerged on that day on Chernyshevskaya Street. The nurse announced what he'd been waiting for and still couldn't really expect,

"Are you Blekhman?"

Samuil went so pale that the nurse got scared and immediately added,

"Don't worry, Blekhman. You now have a son. He's healthy and he weighs three kilograms and three hundred grams."

He jumped into their room without taking off his shoes and barely managed to find New Year's greeting cards on Klara's desk. It wasn't that hard to find them, but he barely had time to look. As for wanting to look, he had even less of that. He grabbed the very first card he could see. It depicted the Old Year with a long white beard and the New Year that looked like a baby. The two Years were raising champagne glasses and smiling at each other. The Old Year was smiling wisely while the New Year had a look of contentment.

"The truth, Klara, is in wine!" Samuil had told her when they were buying this card. "In vino veritas!"

"And this is the kind of father fate has given to my child," Klara had observed.

Samuil, however, had tried to offer an explanation,

"A son should get his first drink of alcohol from his father's hands. A father can do no wrong."

Klara, however, would not budge on this issue.

"The truth," she had said in spite of her husband's passionate embraces, "is to be imbibed with the mother's milk and not with the father's port wine."

"I agree!" said Samuil who was happy with everything. "And after he imbibes and grows up, I will recommend he take a couple of ounces, for purely medical purposes."

Who cares if it was last year or this one? He grabbed the card without thinking twice and wrote something that didn't really matter anymore on it with his impeccably straight letters that refused to bend in any direction. Then he rushed back to visit them and on the way bought some fruit to send to Klara. I arrived too early because the babies were still being fed. Then, finally, they brought me Klara's answer, which sounded just like I expected and it was great because it meant that they were both feeling very well,

"No need to doubt anything. Misha looks just like you. He is red and very ugly, and I love him already. I kiss you both, although I can't kiss either of you for real right now, albeit for different reasons."

Samuil laughed and set out to visit everybody he knew and deliver this most important piece of news in his life. He went to Maria Isaakovna's Engineering House, to Vladimir Fedorovich's Southern Railway Bureau, to Zinovi and Berta's place, and to his parents' house on Dobrokhotova Street. He yelled and sang, grabbed everybody, hugged them, and almost threw them up in the air.

Then he ran back to the hospital again and brought more fruit. It was dark but he didn't notice that because suddenly he saw Klara in the window, and she was holding their son. Samuil started crying and didn't notice that either.

"Misha!!" he yelled so loudly that the crows on the December trees that looked so different from the ones in Arkul turned white out of sheer surprise.

"That's strange," I thought. "He called me this name so many times, but this was the first time he said it."

I wanted to call back but couldn't.

That is, I could, but Samuil didn't hear me. . .

LXIV

She was looking into my notebook that, thanks to her, was turning into a book. She was looking into my notebook and into the window of the trolley-bus where the same ornament made out of strange hieroglyphs was painted as I can see on my own window-pane. She made a wish and smiled, looking at Samuil who was either walking or running down the hospital's alley that emerged onto the dreamy Stalin Boulevard. He was singing a Neapolitan song that disturbed the entire city of Kharkov, tired after that long Thursday. A policeman who suspected the worst approached him and asked him in a voice that, as a policeman, he must have considered very quiet,

"Citizen, are you in your right mind?"

Samuil hugged him and screamed,

"Friend, I just had a son! Can you believe it?"

The policeman was glad that his suspicions hadn't been justified for once.

"Kiss your wife for me," he said. "But try not to wake people up. Everybody has got to go to work tomorrow."

"Brother, I'll kiss her for myself!" Samuil yelled and started singing another Italian song. Now, however, his singing was less loud.

He already knew that I existed while I still had no idea he did.

* * *

Our cities had celebrated Christmas and were getting ready for New Year's, and then for another Christmas.

I closed the notebook that was about to become another book. Thankfully, the notebook refused to close or to end, even though I was sure I'd covered the last page. The notebook remained open, and every word of it asked me not to close it.

Both they and I were waiting for New Year's. They weren't thinking that the fifties were already rushing nobody knew where because they had just been toasting the forties. They weren't thinking about it because they had so many other things to think about, and now they had another person to think about, too.

They were thinking about me, and I couldn't think of them yet. . .

And now yet another New Year's is approaching, and we have traded places.

Only my "yet" has turned into their "already."

I kept looking at the snow stars that were streaming towards me and repeating the same wish. Only it wasn't coming true, probably because there were no more stars left in the skies for this, most important wish of mine. . .

I looked at the river and felt like the captain of our shared unusual vessel. I was thinking about them because if it hadn't been for them, I wouldn't exist and neither would this river or those books, the one in the mother-of-pearl cover that they helped me decipher and that other one that has served as a justification for my notebook.

The notebook that has finally found its name.

My notebook that, without them, would have never transformed into the book that matters the most to me, into a reflection of the manuscript that wasn't created by me.

Of course, I didn't create it.

They did.

Those people whom, God willing, I will once live up to.

www.ingramcontent.com/pod-product-compliance
Lightning Source LLC
Chambersburg PA
CBHW060352080526
44583CB00012B/284